Totalitarianism

Totalitarianism

Michael Curtis

Transaction Books
New Brunswick (U.S.A.) and London (U.K.)

Second Printing 1980

Copyright © 1979 by Transaction, Inc.
New Brunswick, New Jersey 08903

Library of Congress Catalog Number: 78-66238
ISBN: 0-87855-288-X (cloth); 0-87855-688-5 (paper)
Printed in the United States of America

**Library of Congress Cataloging
in Publication Data**

Curtis, Michael, 1923-
    Totalitarianism.

    Includes bibliographical references and index.
    1. Totalitarianism. I. Title.
JC481.C87   321.9   78-66238
ISBN 0-87855-288-X
ISBN 0-87855-688-5 pbk.

Contents

70244

1
Totalitarianism

Political taxonomy is an intellectual endeavor
not to be undertaken lightly. To attempt the classification of political systems, all of which are unique, which have varied historical backgrounds,
different sets of social relationships, are at dissim-
ilar levels of economic modernization, and are in
constant flux, is to enter a thicket of controversy
from which it is difficult to escape unscratched. It
is small satisfaction that biological classification
suffers from similar handicaps. In political discussion, where the number of variables present is
larger, if not necessarily less precise, classification takes on a normative as well as an analytical
character and inevitably becomes controversial.

Is there a genus of political systems called totalitarian, or are these systems simply a subset of the
more historically familiar authoritarian polities?
And can a system called totalitarian change its
political spots and transform itself into a regime of
a different genre?

The concept of totalitarianism has been used by
analysts to suggest a qualitative difference

1

between three regimes—Nazi Germany, Fascist Italy, and the Soviet Union at least until the death of Stalin—and the countless dictatorial systems that have existed throughout history. There are three major problems raised by such a classification. The first is whether the similarities among the three regimes are sufficiently great for them to be encompassed in one species. A corollary of this would be the question of whether some, or all three systems, might more appropriately be classified in a different manner, perhaps as fascist regimes or as mass-movement regimes, or as examples of developmental dictatorship. The second problem is that of deciding if the Soviet Union, the only survivor of the three, has changed its nature as its political leaders have changed. Are the characteristics of Soviet "totalitarianism" still present now, or have there been qualitative differences in the post-Stalin period? The third problem is whether any other political systems can appropriately be regarded as similar enough to the original three to be put into the same category.

THE TOTALITARIAN CONCEPT

The totalitarian concept has been a useful term to typify a particular genre of contemporary regime in an age of mass democracy in which the population can be controlled by a variety of means, especially terror. Dictatorships, despotisms, and autocratic regimes are akin to totalitarian ones in their elitist rule, arbitrary use of political power, minimization of private individual rights, and in their ordered and hierarchical

institutions. Bonapartist systems are similar in
their charismatic leadership, independence of the
executive from any real control, nationalistic
emphasis, appeals to popular support for approval
of policies, and their interest in alleviating social
discontent. Police states have similarities in the
strong intervention of state power and the arbitrary exercise of police power, often including a
secret police.

But these other types of regime not only depend
to a considerable degree on a variety of social
forces such as the army, monarchy, church or business, but also leave whole areas of life untouched
by official control which largely rests on the pas-
sivity of the population. Louis XIV, who asserted
that "Kings are absolute lords and by nature have
complete and free disposition of all wealth . . . to
use . . . according to the general need of their state"
also assumed that subjects have their own individual right of property in particular goods, even if
that right was not an absolute one.[1] Authoritarian
regimes have permitted some free expression of
opinion, if it is not considered destructive of the
regime, and some freedom to enter the economic
market. The analysis of previous authoritarian
systems that argued that the larger the number of
individuals ruled by a tyrant the smaller the part
of the individual which he could dominate, was
valid for historical eras where only a part of the
lives of the individuals was so dominated, and
where the technical implements to do more were
not present.[2] In general authoritarian regimes
rarely are inspired by an integrated, or meaning-

ful, ideology or claim to embody a particular historical destiny.

Totalitarian systems embody not only strong and arbitrary power but also the insistence on conformity of the whole society, mass mobilization, the subjugation of all classes to a dominant political group and attacks on the "enemies" of the system and on their ideology. Resting on mass support and mass movements rather than on the economic and social groups that formed the elite in earlier systems and maintained by a combination of force, indoctrination, and propoganda, the totalitarian regime is tutelary in nature, purporting to incarnate the true and necessary values to give meaning to the lives of its citizens. Such regimes appeared at a historical moment when traditional and religious values have a declining efficacy on individuals and when the state of man in modern democratic systems does not lead to an easy integration into organizations based on the common interest.[3] With the technological controls at its disposal, the regime attempts the implementation of that meaning by the creation of a new society and a new type of citizen. Totalitarianism has meant that the whole community is drawn into the political arena, elections are contrived, and the citizens are mobilized for the purposes of the regime. Though the Reichstag in Nazi Germany was a powerless institution it was dissolved and reelected four times in five years.

The aphorism of Dostoevsky, "all things are permitted," pervades the experience of the three systems. They have been termed "totalitarian" in the light of their claim that no interest falls outside the embrace of the state or the wielders of power, that the purposes of individuals, groups, and society are subordinate to those of the state, that the state or ruling group monopolizes decision-making, that all opposition is prohibited, that there are no independent expressions of public opinion, that there is no constitutional form of self-government, and that there are few or no limits on the rulers. The only goals are those defined by the state to which all social organs were subject. Law as a constraint on government, or, on the amount of suffering the rulers are prepared to inflict, or, as the protection of individual rights against official action virtually disappeared. Political activity is viewed in terms of ultimate objectives rather than as the empirical attempt to solve problems. The official creed replaces that of orthodox religion and is transformed into a secular faith claiming absolute loyalty and brooking no challenge to the principles of its liturgy.

If politics is organized dispute about the use of power, involving choices among competing values and persons, then totalitarianism is the negation of politics in its lack of any real freedom or choice, in its claim to create definitive social conditions,[4] and in its demand to control both social life and individual conscience in order to create a new type of man. The distinctiveness of totalitarianism arises, as Orwell argued, in the effort to control thoughts and emotions as well as actions. Its novelty is in the more efficient technological devices, the mass media, the skilled personnel, and the mass support available for coercion, manipulation, and indoctrination of whole populations to implement the perceived truth or objectives and to bring about the desired changes in thought and action.

The concept of "totalitarianism" appeared in Italy in 1924 and 1925 with the phrase "uno stato totalitario" coined by Gentile on behalf of Mussolini. The intellectual pedigree of the idea can be traced back to the Greeks.[5] For Plato, control over the polity would extend not only to political arrangements, literary censorship, and personal beliefs, but also to music, architecture, gymnastics, and dress. But the concept of plebiscitary democracy that has been a constant element in radical thought since the French Revolution[6] stems from Rousseau's idea of the general will as the will of the people, particularly in the distorted form expounded by Robespierre and St. Just who called for a despotism of freedom against tyranny. The general will for Rousseau would achieve its purest expression "when all citizens confront the state as individuals and are not bound together in lesser associations." Totalitarianism draws from this fount the justification that opponents can be regarded as enemies of the general will and of the people and can be eliminated, that terror is necessary to fulfill historical destiny, and that an individual who tried, either actively or passively, to exclude himself from the activities of the community had to be destroyed.

Contemporary analysts who have thought the concept of totalitarianism valuable have defined it, or tried to list characteristics of totalitarian systems, in somewhat different ways. The fact that the definitions vary does not or should not of itself lead to a denial of the distinctiveness of the regimes analyzed, nor to the conclusion that the concept lacks utility. Nor is it pertinent to argue, as does Marcuse[7] among others, that manipulation is common to all systems and that nonterroristic economic-technological coordination, operating through the manipulation of needs by vested interests, is common to the Western world. Equally erroneous is the argument familiar in the late 1960s that the use of the concept is simply a weapon in the Cold War of the post World War II period, utilitized at a particular moment for opposition to or discrediting of communism.[8] The writings of Deutscher, Duverger, Orwell, Neumann, and Borkenau, among others, not to mention the opinions on the similarity of Bolshevism and Fascism held by Lloyd George in 1923 and by Luigi Sturzo and Francesco Nitti[9] who saw them as the two integral rebuttals of the liberal system and democracy in 1926, dispel such a view as counterpolemic of its own.

Totalitarianism has in fact been a useful term, applicable to political systems of a certain genre. For analytical purposes it is worthwhile to list the key variables as they appear in the literature on the subject:

1. An official and exclusive ideology or set of convictions to which the society is to be committed and which will be the basis for a new type of political and social order and for a new type of man.

2. Monopoly control, not only over political, economic, social, and cultural behavior, but also over private life and personal thought, to produce total conformity of the whole society.

3. The use of terror, concentration camps, and a political police force to help produce that conformity and to pose a permanent threat against the individual.

4. A hierarchically organized one-party system or movement regime, from which pluralism on Western democratic lines is absent.

5. The subordination of private interests to and on behalf of the public or collective interest through which the reality of the individual is affirmed.

6. As a corollary, a stress on centralization of power, unity, and integration, with opposition or even dissent regarded as an offence.

7. The removal of legal limits on the wielders of power.

8. Monopoly control of the media of communication and the educational and the cultural process, in order to mobilize the society.

9. The absence of meaningful free elections.

10. Monopoly control over weapons and force.

11. Denial of the right of citizens to travel abroad, and sometimes internally, at will.

12. A centrally planned economy in which production is stressed and consumption con-

trolled to provide accumulation of capital for investment purposes.

13. The preeminence of an individual ruler whose personal dictatorship may be the key factor in the nature of the regime.

2

The Process of Becoming Totalitarian

If one accepts these key characteristics as defining totalitarian regimes, the initial problem in analysis of totalitarianism is one common in the social sciences: to what extent can reliable generalization be made about the experience of a number of finite, unique, and historically specific systems? Are there sufficient similarities of a qualitative nature to allow Nazi Germany, Fascist Italy, and the Soviet Union under Stalin to be regarded as common members of the same political species?

It must be admitted that there were significant differences in the operation and experience of the three systems. They did not all exhibit the key characteristics to the same degree: in Italy some of them were hardly present at all. They took different periods of time to reach the stage of monopolistic political control in which all opposition, actual or potential, had been eliminated and terror became the dominant element in the system. Italy and Germany were more conscious advocates of a totalitarian conception of politics than was the Soviet Union. The widely different political cultures of the countries led to considerable variation in the implementation of common ideas. In all the regimes there was great discrepancy, sometimes even an inverse relationship, between ideology and beliefs and resulting practice. The theory itself, especially its implication of monolithic entities, is not always borne out by the political reality. Nevertheless, even admitting all this, there does remain sufficiently similar political experience and style, particularly in the use of terror, the role of the dictator, and the mobilization of the population, to allow the three systems to be placed in a common classification.

In Italy, Mussolini had decided as early as September 20, 1922, that "we shall leave the monarchical institution on our side, outside our scope," and earlier, on November 7, 1921, that "we are liberal in economic affairs." In his March 1923 speech to the International Chamber of Commerce he declared that "the state must give up its economic functions with which it is unable to cope." Freedom of the press was not curbed until 1924 and academic freedom not until 1931. The decisive moment of Fascism came on January 3, 1925, after the political difficulties caused by the murder of Matteotti, when Mussolini declared, "I, and I alone, assume the political, moral and historical responsibility for all that happened."

Between 1925 and 1927 all opposition parties were suppressed, their leaders killed or arrested or exiled. The free trade unions were abolished and the fascist unions given a monopoly. Concentration camps were started and the death sentence imposed for political offences. In 1928 the Chamber of Deputies was dissolved and replaced by a body nominated by the Grand Council of Fascism. Though general unified cultural controls were not imposed until the mid 1930s, the Fascist political monopoly was now in force.

The Nazi system began in more ruthless fashion. The February 1933 law enabled the police to imprison people suspected of treasonable intentions as well as overt activity. By the Enabling Act of March, 1933, Hitler could promulgate decrees without reference to the legislature. Yet even then it was only with the dismissal of conservatives like Schacht, von Blomberg, von Fritsch, and von Neurath in 1937 and 1938, that the Nazis assumed control over the economy, the army, and the diplomatic service. Not until the war was the economy fully mobilized.

In the Soviet Union, monopolistic command resulted from the control of the state by the ruling party, the elimination of all other parties in 1921, the banning of factions within the party by the tenth party Congress in the same year, the control over the trade unions and social organzizations, the prohibition of the church from all social and educational activity and its restriction to religious ritual.[10] There is wide difference of opinion on the responsibility of Lenin for the totalitarianism of the Stalinist years, from Solzhenitsyn,[11] who

argues that Stalinism inevitably resulted from
Lenin's activities and declaration in January 1918
of the need "to purge the Russian land of all harm-
ful insects," and his mandate in a telegram of
August 1918 that "doubtful" elements should be
put in a concentration camp, to Medvedev, who
holds that Stalinism was a complete perversion of
Lenin's ideas, and that Stalin acted in defiance of
Lenin's instructions.[12]

It was Lenin who stressed the necessity of a dictatorship of the proletariat and who devised the
idea of a dictatorship of the party led by the Central Committee in *What is to be Done?* in 1902. On
October 10, 1920, he defined dictatorship as "un-
limited power." Early in power he advocated the
use of terror against opponents, reintroducing the
death penalty and organizing in 1917 the Cheka,
which had wide discretionary powers of arrest
which could not be appealed, and which executed
without trial about 8,000 people and arrested at
least 90,000 others including Tsarist officials,
Constitutional Democrats, Social Revolutionaries, Mensheviks, anarchists, and the rebellious
Kronstadt sailors. He dispersed the newly elected
Constituent Assembly against the views of the
Central Committee of his party. At the ninth party
Congress in April 1920 it was decided to subordinate the trade unions to the party organization. In
1921 over 170,000 members were purged from the
party. By 1923 the Soviet Union was being condemned at the Socialist International meeting in
Hamburg as terrorist dictatorship.[13]

But restraints were present in the Leninist
period. Agriculture and, after 1921, much small

scale industry and distribution were dominated by market considerations or in private hands. The change from the NEP to a socialist society would be for Lenin an evolutionary one which required the education of the population.[14] Though censorship was severe under Lenin there was still considerable freedom of expression in politics, as well as in the arts and in science, without the imposition of a compulsory authoritative line. Lenin may personally have had little regard for modernism in literature and art and criticized a poem by Mayakovsky as "errant nonsense, stupidity and pretentiousness," but he refrained from imposing his personal views on others.[15] Medvedev even argues that the tenth party Congress in 1921, while banning factions, also called for a more regular publication of discussion bulletins and special collections of documents, and that at the ninth All-Russian party Conference in September 1920 there was a call for more extensive criticism within the party of both local and central party institutions.[16] By contrast, under Stalin by 1929 there were no nonparty publications allowed nor any privately owned publishing houses.

Lenin was unmistakenly the dominant political figure, but the Soviet political oligarchy embraced a central committee containing over forty people, the Council of People's Commissars, the executive machinery of the party, the trade unions, official organs and local party organizations, all of which exercized a certain degree of power.[17] Lenin thought of the dictatorship as temporary in nature. Just before his death in 1924, Lenin optimistically but unprophetically told Maxim Gorky that "the young will have much happier lives than we had . . . There will not be much cruelty in their lives."

THE USE OF TERROR

If Lenin was intolerant and sometimes brutal and ruthless, he lacked the sadism, vengefulness, and paranoia of Stalin. There was a plausible and understandable, if not acceptable, rationale for Lenin's intolerance toward, and elimination of, political opponents and use of terror in his attempt to consolidate the revolution, to overcome the division of the civil war, to arrest the widespread famine, and to end the actuality or threat of foreign intervention. It could be argued that the ban imposed by the tenth party Congress in 1921 on party factions and groups which had not been forbidden until then was regarded by Lenin as a temporary measure. There was far less plausibility to, if considerable acceptance of, Stalin's argument from the late 1920s until he died that dictatorship was necessary to safeguard the revolution and to protect the Soviet Union from capitalist encirclement.

If there is any single characteristic that differentiates totalitarian systems from others in time and in space, it is the extreme use of terror. Arendt, Friedrich, Fainsod, Neumann, all have seen terror as a crucial feature of totalitarian regimes. Certainly this is valid as a commentary on the Nazi and Stalinist experiences. Yet the Italian system might more appropriately be regarded as a police state rather than as one based on terror. In 1927

OVRA, the political police force, was organized to eliminate political opposition. The police could authorize the existence of associations, and confinement could be imposed on those suspected of intention to engage in subversive activity. But the OVRA rarely tortured; the threat of coercion usually sufficed to obtain compliance. Censorship varied in intensity. Between 1926 and 1943 about 21,000 people were brought before special courts, some 10,000 people were imprisoned without trial, and twenty-five opponents were killed.

There was a sharp difference in severity between the Fascist and Nazi regimes, explicable in terms of their different objectives, the fanaticism of their doctrines, the vastly different political cultures, and the difference in their bureaucratic machines. It took Fascism over four years to suppress political parties; in Germany such suppression was immediate. In April 1939 there were over 300,000 in prisons and concentration camps for political reasons. In 1945 there were 714,000 in concentration camps guarded by 40,000 SS men. By the end of the regime at least 10 million and probably 12 million had been murdered. The Holocaust has become the chief memory of Nazism.

In the Soviet Union the terror began under Lenin, who in 1918 urged the need for "purging the Russian land" as if terror were a kind of political hygiene. The purpose of terrorism, said Lenin, was to terrify. Torture, public confession, self abasement occurred. Under Lenin, Maria Spiridonova, who broke with him after Brest-Litovsk, was confined to a mental hospital. Even then the means employed—the trial of Social Revolutionaries in 1922 designed to destroy their party, the agents provacateurs used against opponents, the false accusations against the Kronstadt rebels in 1921—caused concern even to admirers like Gorky. Lenin himself became increasingly aware of the dangers of the strong power in the hands of the Cheka, which in 1922 was transformed into the OGPU, to deal only with dangerous crimes against the state such as counterrevolution and espionage. He was aware, as he wrote in his letter to the twelfth party Congress, just before his death, of the need to change a number of things in the political system.

But under his successor the power of the secret police was vastly increased. Its powers were no longer limited to a concern with crimes of a specific nature but were extended to anyone declared "a socially dangerous person" which was definable as anyone not completely accepting the Stalinist position at any moment. Internal enemies of this kind would first be physically eliminated and then historically expunged to become nonpersons. In the show trials at which they are condemned the victims appear as irremediable.[18] Under Stalin the use of terror, with the illegal arrests, arbitrary use of coercion and brutality against individuals and groups, use of torture, creation of a prison camp system, psychological as well as physical fear, and destruction of his own party, has been explained in different ways. Some relate it to Tsarist "exceptional laws" and absolutist behavior patterns, which made brutality a significant part of Russian political culture. The Russian

Orthodox tradition of icons, relics of saints, and processions appears as the cultural ancestry of Soviet imagery, cult of the leader and official liturgy in which demons and saboteurs were named in order to be exorcized. The models of Ivan IV, Peter the Great, and the Grand Dukes of Moscow who created a centralized bureaucracy and a system in which all citizens were liable for state service in some form, and which was responsible for a variety of social activities, were combined by Stalin with those elements of Leninism emphasizing revolutionary spirit and will, class struggle, dictatorship of the proletariat, terror and summary justice.[19]

It has been more evident, however, with the accumulating information about the labor camps, that the slave labor employed was a reinforcing element in the employment of terror because of the economic gains from the use of cheap or free labor in the building of factories, railroads and dams, and construction projects in general. Labor camps accounted for 12 percent of all Soviet timber cut, for 22 percent of the building of the country's railroads, and for 75 percent of the gold mined. Medvedev argues that about 15 percent of the most important scientific projects and not less than 50 percent of atomic energy research was conducted in special MGB and MVD institutes by political prisoners who had been scientists and specialists.[20] The political police not only administered the labor camps but also supervised the economy to some degree through its concern over the thefts. The NKVD, the renamed OGPU, became perhaps the largest employer of labor in the country.

More influential, if pernicious, has been the argument that the economic backwardness of Russia, the low level of development, the need for forced collectivization of agriculture to overcome the kulaks in order to amass capital for industrialization, made terror and "the revolution from above, on the initiative of the state" necessary. Attractive though this thesis has been to defenders of the regime as well as to some leaders of developing countries, it does not account for the Leningrad party purge after the murder of Kirov in 1934, for acts such as the massacre of over 10,000 Ukrainians in Vinnytsia in 1937-38, or, of over 4,000 Polish officers in the Katyn Forest in 1940, nor for the brutality shown to engineers, socialists, minorities, religious people, and to returning prisoners of war after World War II, especially the 2 million people who had been unwillingly sent back to the Soviet Union after being freed or released from internment in Western Europe after the end of the war,[21] nor for the killing of a minimum of 20 million,[22] nor for the granting of extraordinary powers to the NKVD to destroy "the enemies of the people." Solzhenitsyn has calculated that from 1917 to 1953 between 40 and 50 million went through the prison and labor camps.

The Stalinist terror has been defended, as by Merleau-Ponty, as being necessary for the consolidation of proletarian dictatorship. In this view Stalinism is a true derivative of Marxism which is "*the* philosophy of history" and which must be accepted if one is not "to block out historical reason."[23] Its uniqueness has been minimized by the argument that some form of political terror is present in all societies and that the Stalinist era was different only in degree. A case might be made that the first major show trial, of industrial specialists in 1930, may have had a rationale for Stalin in preventing any possibility of the technical intelligentsia's exercising a greater political role in the Soviet Union or forming a political coalition with the Bukharin group.[24] One might argue that Stalin saw himself as the true defender of the revolution and disciple of Lenin, attributing absolute value to Marxist ideology and believing that nothing must take precedence over the interests of the party as interpreted by him. In his secret speech in 1956 Khrushchev, while denouncing Stalin's crimes, nevertheless explained that "we cannot say that these were the deeds of a despot. Stalin considered this should be done in the interest of the party, of the working masses, in the name of the defence of the revolution's gains." Over 60 percent of the party membership of 1933 had disappeared by 1939, and some 279,000 were expelled from the party in 1937-38. One of the few achievements was the increase in the number of specialists in the party.[25]

Some analysts have tended to see Stalin's role as an agent of history. For E. H. Carr, Stalin's objectives were dictated "by the dynamic force inherent in the revolution itself" and his actions seen as those of "the great executor of revolutionary policy." Deutscher explains that Stalin, acting under the overwhelming pressure of events to meet "the grave social crisis" at the end of the 1920s undertook and accomplished "the second revolution" of collectivization and industrialization in the 1930's.[26]

But the Stalinist terror was not only excessive and extreme within the Soviet system; it was highly personal in nature, the result of individual paranoia, ambition, vanity, or envy. By the mid-1920s there remained critics of the regime but there were no dangerous internal enemies. Yet at the seventeenth party Congress in January 1934 Stalin still warned of the "enemies both internal and external." Stalin's argument, logically absurd though it was, that the remaining elements of the defeated exploited classes could become more desperate and the class struggle would intensify as the Soviet Union became more successful, should not have applied to the party itself. Even Hitler, apart from the Röhm purge and the night of the long knives in 1934 and his execution of those implicated in the attempt on his life of July 1944, did not murder members of his own party or officials. But through the OGPU and the NKVD Stalin extended the terror to the party itself as well as to the general populace. Between 1936 and 1938 over one million party members were killed by Stalin: in his *History of the Communist Party: Short Course,* he calls them "white-guard pygmies, whose strength was no more than a gnat." Some seventy-five percent of the governing class of the country was purged.[27] By 1939 Stalin had murdered 110 of the 139 members and candidate members of the Central Committee of the party elected at the seventeenth congress in 1934. The same fate was suffered by most of the Commission of Party Control. The one party system, as Tucker has argued, became the one person system.[28] The development of Stalinism from the social upheaval of 1929-23 to its complete triumph by 1936 meant the wrecking of earlier real achievements.[29]

There is legitimate difference of opinion on the nature of the contemporary Soviet Union. The executions do not now roll in the dictator's mouth. Since it is apparent that terror has been reduced in the post-Stalin period, the conclusion has been drawn that the system can no longer accurately be described as totalitarian. Under Khruschev the Special Boards of the MVD were abolished and more emphasis put on social pressure, material incentives, and the comrade's courts to obtain compliance. Yet the apparatus of terror has not been dismantled. The gulag system still exists, political police still watch the populace, and censorship has varied in its thoroughness. Most surprisingly, psychiatry has been seriously abused by the KGB, mental hospitals have been used as political prisons, and disagreement with the nature or policies of the Soviet system seen as a symptom of insanity. The thaw in the Soviet Union following the death of Stalin, which led many observers to argue that totalitarianism was a transitory phenomenon, has been succeeded by a relative refreezing.

3
Development and Dictatorship

Was Stalin really necessary? It is ironic that for all Stalin's supposed concern about the danger of external enemies, his foreign policy was disastrous, leading indirectly to Hitler's accession to power and almost to German victory over the Soviet Union in World War II. Internally the terror, with its murders, civil war against the peasants, and collectivization of 125 million peasants, was counterproductive both materially and ideologically. The history of the Soviet Union would seem to suggest that forced collectivization of agriculture and the extraordinary accompanying violence was not necessary to increase industrialization. On the contrary, it was a disaster from which the country has still not fully recovered. No net resources were contributed to the industrial sector and famine was created, with the destruction of at least 10 million cows and 17 million horses by 1932.[30]

Medvedev has calculated that between 4 and 5 million died of starvation in the Ukraine alone. By 1934 there was a 22 percent decline in farm output. Between 1913 and 1953 average farm yields in the Soviet Union did not increase and were only one-third of the yields in other European countries. Collectivization and the elimination of kulaks were both essential to Stalin to bring about the necessary changes in the relations of production. A member of the kolkhoz could not move to the city or another district without permission.[31] The kolkhoz had no real autonomy of its own; management was imposed on it. The kulaks, the personification of the peasant mode of production, who constituted a class that Stalin thought would not accept socialism, were condemned to liquidation. Stalin left agriculture weaker than before, a population terrorized, about 10 million peasants murdered and a party leadership decimated. Robert Conquest's witticism is pertinent: "Stalinism is one way of attaining industrialization, just as cannibalism is one way of attaining a high protein diet."

Ideologically, terror led to the deification of the despot, the elimination of free expression in the party, the heightened power of the state, the revival of Russian nationalism, outbreaks of anti-Semitism, the repeal of progressive social legislation benefiting workers, women, school children, and minority cultures, to greater social stratification and to the reversal of the trend toward egalitarianism.[32] Draconian laws applied even to children: in 1935 children over twelve were made subject to criminal charges, the penalty for which included death. The parallel with a Tsarist "revolution from above" is an insufficient characterization. The Stalinist period can be viewed as a return to serfdom in which the peasants were deprived of rights, tied to the collective farms by an internal passport system and made responsible for providing a minimum amount of work and supplies to the state.[33] Bukharin called it "military-feudal exploitation of the peasantry." But the use of forced labor for such activities as road building and timber cutting and the internal transfer of enormous numbers of people vastly exceeded anything in Tsarist history.

Nevertheless, the idea of forced development has been regarded as crucial to the totalitarian regimes. Analysts like Russell and Borkenau early characterized the systems as one party dictatorships aiming at rapid industrialization and economic modernization for which economic sacrifices were necessary.[34] More recently, Robert Tucker has suggested that the systems might be included under the rubric of revolutionary mass movement regimes under single party auspices. These regimes carry on revolutionary struggles against internal or external opponents in the name of national renovation or expansion, and they control the political, social, and economic life of the country.[35] Elsewhere, Tucker argues that the communist revolution is one of underdevelopment both in the sense that it occurs in a setting of underdevelopment and that it becomes the basis for efforts to overcome that underdevelopment.[36]

In this and similar views, the three systems appear as influential examples of a world wide tendency of movements, led by elites under a single party dictatorship dominated by a leader, that mobilize the population, that appeal for action on behalf of the whole community, and that stress the necessity for strong state power to raise productivity and modernize their systems. The regimes would exemplify what Apter has called "mobilization systems."[37]

Certainly the Soviet Union, especially in the NEP period, can be perceived from this perspective. In 1924 Stalin stated that the principal task of socialism, the organization of socialist production, had still to be fulfilled.[38] Between 1925 and 1928[39] he spoke of the need to accumulate capital through low wages to increase electrification, to apply machines to agriculture on a mass scale and to create a "new technical basis of modern large-scale production" to beat the internal enemy. In the *Economic Problems of Socialism* written at the end of his life, Stalin argued that the basic economic law requires "the continuous expansion and perfection of social production on the basis of higher techniques." To bring the "lagging relations of production into conformity with the character of the productive forces" action must be taken which would include greater stress on farms as public property, the replacement of commodity circulation by a "system of products-exchange, and by the expansion of the production of the means of production."

But the actions of Stalin were as counterproductive in industry as they were in agriculture. Between 1929 and 1932, in spite of the increase in investment in heavy industry by over 580 percent and in the labor force by 89 percent, industrial output per worker declined by about 10 percent a year. Even in steel production, the most favored enterprise, total output increased by only 2 percent in the same period.[40] By 1932 real per capita income had dropped to about half of the 1928 level. It seems paradoxical to use the term "modernization" to categorize Stalinism with this poor productive performance, with its return to Tsarist barbarism, emphasis on Russian rather than on Soviet culture, and employment of strong state power unless the term is simply equated with greater industrialization.[41]

In his report to the sixteenth Congress in 1930, Stalin explained the need for the "strengthening of the dictatorship of the proletariat, which is the mightiest and strongest state power that has ever existed." That power would be responsible, inter alia, for building up heavy industry for national defense, agricultural collectivism, and for control of consumption and markets. In the post-Stalin period the Soviet Union still emphasizes the increase in production and in economic productivity as its major goals.[42] In a country that still insists on the meaningfulness of its ideology, an inherent contradiction between utopian goals and practical necessity is deepening. The urgent desire to attain modernity, requiring increasing emphasis on economic man and material needs, conflicts with the ultimate objective of a classless society in which disagreeable personal traits such as ambition and avarice are to have vanished.[43]

The struggle to achieve a developed economy has also been seen by some as the most approp-

riate way to analyze Italian Fascism, for Mussolini had a serious commitment to the maintenance
and expansion of the nation's productive capacity
as well as to the resurgence of the Italian state.[44]
Symbolically, he changed the subtitle of his news-
paper in 1918 from "A Socialist Daily" to "A Daily
of Combatants and Producers." Between 1922 and
1938, Gregor argues, Fascist Italy became an economically mature society.[45] The industrial sector
expanded and steel production increased.

Fascism has thus been analyzed as a developmental dictatorship in which the capital accumulation necessary for industrial expansion was
obtained by suppressing labor unrest and
demands, by controlling consumption, and by
promoting austerity. The problem with this argument is that economic growth was in fact slower
during most of the Fascist era than both earlier
and later.[46] In 1938 only one-third of total national
income was derived from the industrial sector.
There was a slow increase in industrial
employment—24 percent of workers in 1921 and 28
percent in 1936—and a slow decrease in the pro-
portion of agricultural workers—56 percent in
1921 and 48 percent in 1936.[47] No substantial
increase occurred in the technologically more progressive branches of industry. When Bottai, Minister of Corporations, tried to plan, he was
removed by Mussolini. Indeed, Mussolini engaged
in a back to the rural areas crusade in the 1930s.

In any case, Mussolini was more preoccupied
with, and gave higher priority to, territorial
expansion and military power than to the trans-
formation of the economic and social structure of

Italy. The drive for autarky was wasteful. Social and economic stability was achieved at the expense of mobility and dynamism.[48] Italian Fascism, administratively inefficient and corrupt, heedless of true economic costs, concerned with political rather than with economic ends, cannot be regarded as the paradigm of modernization, in spite of the symbolic value of Mussolini's playing the role of racing driver or pilot appealing to the modern spirit.

There are two final difficulties about the concept of developmental dictatorship. One is that it tends to neglect, or certainly to minimize, the significance of communism or ideological conviction in the Soviet Union as well as the role of Stalin. The other is that it is not applicable to Germany, already a highly industrialized and politically developed system under Weimar. Other explanations for dictatorship there, such as the German social system, historical background, political traditions or the influence of German political ideas, then become necessary, if the inherent dictatorial nature of Nazism is not in itself found sufficient. Attention has therefore also been focused on the German character, distinguished by force, aggression or destruction, or on the Prussian tradition with its ideal of service to the state, militarism and authoritarian disdain for inferiors, or on the inheritance of bellicose nationalism.

4
The Dictator

Next to terror the most significant defining characteristic of totalitarianism and the most important common feature of the three systems in practice was the role of the supreme leader. In Italy, Mussolini emerged as a dictator after the January 3, 1925 speech in which he assumed "the political, moral, and historical responsibility for all that has happened." Laws passed in 1925 and 1926 allowed him to appoint and dismiss ministers at will and to legislate by decree. In 1929 he occupied nine ministries himself, a fragmentation of effort hardly likely to result in efficient administration or effective control; at the end in 1943 he still held five ministries.

Mussolini consolidated his hold over and established his independence of the Fascist party. The former squadristi leaders were tamed, and the paramilitary militia remained under his direct orders. He approved the expulsion by Turati, the new party secretary in 1926, of over 7,000 members. Fascist publications that he regarded as

33

too critical were suppressed. Individuals he envis-
aged as potential rivals—Rocco, Balbo, Bottai,
and Grandi in turn—were dismissed. The Grand
Council, theoretically the supreme deliberative
organ of the state after 1928, met irregularly; he
called it 139 times between 1922 and 1932, but only
forty-seven times in the remaining eleven years of
the regime.

The cult of the Duce, as sex symbol as well as
political leader, became the chief feature of the
regime.[49] In addition to Duce, Mussolini was also
Head of the government, Prime Minister, origina-
tor of decree laws, effective head of all the military,
political, and economic institutions of the regime,
Commander of the militia, head of the Grand
Council of Fascism, and Grand Marshal of the
armed forces of the nation. Not surprisingly, he
could be addressed in these words: "Tu sei
l'Italia."

Yet Mussolini was different from Hitler and
Stalin in a number of ways. He himself quipped
that he was the most disobeyed dictator in history.
Although brutal he was less ruthless than his two
counterparts. Typically, Goebbels expressed his
disappointment that Mussolini had not wreaked
full vengeance on his betrayers in the Grand
Council in 1943: "He is not a revolutionary like the
Führer or Stalin."[50] In addition, he was always
faced by overt or potential challenge, especially by
the ras, the powerful provincial party bosses who
imposed order and ended political opposition in
their areas through a mixture of coercion and
patronage. Throughout his political life Mussolini
was a tactician, often cynical in nature, chame-
leonlike in his ability to appeal to all groups,

manipulating the different factions in the party to minimize the power of each, making concessions to different interests, alternating between support for urban fascism and populism in rural areas. He was more a mediator than a formulator, or imposer, of a point of view.

Indeed, it is doubtful that he had a point of view beyond political survival. His internal policy was essentially the preservation of order. His foreign policy was dictated more by considerations of prestige, progaganda, and public statements than by coherent programs. He became, as Smith argues, the prisoners of the slogans he mouthed.[51]

Mussolini was never quite sure what role to play. Symbolically, the civilian clothes of the 1920s were followed by military garb in the 1930s. He acted the part of the Roman condottiere, adopting not only the title of Duce, but also the Roman symbols (fasces and eagle), the Roman salute and step, and the celebration of Labor Day on April 21, the anniversary of the foundation of Rome. De Felice suggests that even the stress on Romanness may have been due more to the obsession of Margherita Sarfatti about the subject than to his own views.[52] More emphasis was put on patriotism and loyalty to the state than on any Fascist principles. But from Barzini's description of him in 1932—"He wore a white yachting cap, a wing collar, the double-breasted jacket of a businessman, grey-green army breeches, and black boots"[53]—it is difficult to regard him as a serious leader rather than a buffoon or adventurer.

Nevertheless, there were many who believed the slogan that "Mussolini is always right" (Mussolini ha sempre ragione). Gentile, who always

spoke of Fascism as a new spirit, believed that
Mussolini had "the privilege of genius" and incar-
nated "a moral force which springs from the absolute faith which he . . . has in his own ideas and the
providential mission that he is destined to fulfill
for his country and from the great humanity of his
soul."[54] But the myth of the omnipotence of Mussolini was always secondary to that of the Roman
Empire, just as the greatness of Stalin was pur-
portedly secondary to the myth of revolutionary
Marxism or of social justice.

The dominating concept, the basic myth in the
Nazi experience was the indisputable authority of
Hitler. In 1941 Goebbels was to claim that he had
created the myth of the Führer and had given
Hitler the halo of infallibility. In fact as early as
July 1921, Hitler successfully demanded the position of first chairman of the NSDAP (the National
Socialist German Worker's Party) with dictatorial
powers. From that point on, the movement became
less a party than a group of his followers, a holy
order to carry out his commands. In 1925 Hitler
forced the Nazi members to cut their ties to other
paramilitary groups; in 1926 he insisted on the
separate identity of his movement from the völ-
kisch movement. By 1926, when the party program was made an "unalterable" document, it
was evident that final decision making power over
programs, propaganda, administration, and
organization were in his hands.

The key personnel in the party were appointed
by and removed by Hitler. The Gauleiters, all personally loyal to Hitler, were his agents in their territorial areas.[55] He decided who should be a

candidate and for what office. His control over the
central office in Munich, which he wanted maintained as the headquarters of the movement, made
the regions subordinate to centralized decision
making in which the Reich party treasurer and the
Reich propaganda leader (Goebbels) would be his
valuable assistants. The party courts, established
in 1921 and reorganized in 1926, provided another
vehicle through which he could enforce
discipline.[56]

At no point in his career would Hitler tolerate
the creation or existence of organizations that
might diminish his personal authority or leadership. For this reason he opposed the creation of
Nazi unions between 1926 and 1928. By 1930 all
significant decisions were in the hands of Hitler,
to whom a large number of officials reported
directly. The chores of administration, always
unpleasant to him, forced him to establish a unit
under Hess that spoke in his name. Administrative power was delegated to subordinates with the
understanding that Hitler could always interfere
personally.

This preeminence was based partly on his
apparent charisma. Even quite recently, Speer
has written of Hitler's effect on him, of the extraordinary changes of mood and of the force of the personality.[57] But mostly Hitler's domination
resulted from the acceptance by others as well as
by himself of his infallibility of judgment, of his
role as the agent of history, of his authority as the
maker of policy which would be obeyed automati-
cally, and of his organizational leadership, which
could decide on the allocation of authority to be

accorded to subordinates or "derivative agents."[58]
The will of Hitler was equated with that of
Providence.

The highly personal relationship between the
leader and his followers was changed into an
organizational one in the disciplined hierarchical
movement. The Führerprinzip existed long before
Hitler came to power. The dominating principle of
party operation was adherence to the will of
Hitler, irrespective of doctrinal programs. In 1930
he managed to overcome the SA and its leader,
Franz von Pfeffer, by converting the difference
over the role of the SA into a question of personal
loyalty to himself. Within the party, factions did
not organize against Hitler but sought his support
in a dispute;[59] he remained above factional conflicts. For Hitler, political factions could espouse
different positions, provided they remained loyal
to him as final arbiter: Otto Strasser in 1930 and
Gregor Strasser in 1932 were ousted for defying
this cardinal principle.

Hitler's control over the Nazi movement was
complete from the beginning in the early 1920s.
From 1934, after he succeeded Hindenberg as
President and Commander-in-Chief, and after the
1933 civil service law, he was formally in control of
both the executive and legislative power of the
state. On July 13, 1934, after the murders of Röhm
and other leading figures, Hitler declared he was
"responsible for the fate of the German people and
thereby I became the supreme judge of the German
people." In 1938 he took over formal control of the
War Ministry, and in 1941 assumed direct command of the army. Major military decisions such

as the 1936 remilitarization of the Rhineland and
the declaration of war against the United States
were taken against the advice or even the knowledge of the army. During the war, according to a
British general, Hitler rarely listened to his military advisers but directed military strategy
alone.[60] By an April 1942 decree he became the
judge of all German actions. At his disposal were
the Reich Chancellery, which largely replaced the
Cabinet officers, the Presidential Chancellery,
and the Führer Chancellery, which under Bormann concerned itself with party affairs. He was
protected not only by the SS generally, which was
under his authority alone, but also by a special
guard under Dietrich, which swore an oath of personal loyalty to him and which was completely at
his disposal.

Hitler was seen as the source of political legiti-
macy. All public authority both in the state and in
the movement stemmed from the Führer. "Our
constitution" said Hans Frank, the Minister of
Justice, "is the will of the Führer." He was the sole
representative of the people and the embodiment
of its total unity.[61] The myth of Hitler replaced the
need for a program or a coherent political theory.
while in power the derivative agents—the Gauleiters (provincial party leaders), the Reichsleiters
(divisional heads of the movement's administration), the heads of the paramilitary organizations,
and others—all acted on the basis of personal loyalty. Particular posts often were not given clear
powers but depended on Hitler's discretion for
their activities. He sometimes gave different people and departments identical or similar tasks or

appointed two or more rivals for a particular job. All major personnel appointments were controlled by Hitler, or by Hess on his behalf.

All Nazi leaders competed with each other for Hitler's favors, or support for programs, in a series of feuds and alliances formed for tractical purposes. The most important criterion for political success was access to Hitler. The confusing multitude of offices and leaders led to bitter jurisdictional and power struggles. But the major policies were made by Hitler, the artist manqué playing his role on the world stage. His foreign and military policy was a compound of conviction and opportunism, but his major aims—the elimination of Jews, the expansion for lebensraum, the struggle against Bolshevism—determined the thrust of his actions.

A willingness to use extreme violence underlaid all Hitler's action and policies. Not only was he prepared to liquidate the Jewish population of Europe so that the continent would be rid "of the Jewish plague," he also authorized the execution of the whole male population of Stalingrad, agreed to the murders of the Polish intelligentsia, the shooting of Russian prisoners or war and the killing of fifty hostages for every German killed by civilians.

Can one ever fathom human motivation? The very extremism of Hitler's behavior and views makes one wary about assessing the roots of his actions. Bullock saw him as primarily motivated by a will to power in its crudest form.[62] Fest, in his psychological approach, sees the central factor as fear—fear of being racially overwhelmed and of

falling in social scale.[63] Waite argues that anti-
Semitism was almost the organizing principle of
his life and that his hatred of Jews prevented him
from becoming psychotic. But Waite also sees
Hitler as both "a mentally deranged human being
and a consummately skillful politician of high
intelligence," and as a border-line personality
with a compulsive need for destruction.[64] Was he a
self-deluded prophet, believing he possessed the
means of salvation for Germany? Or a destructive
force, inflamed by hatred of contemporary civili-
zation and of a bourgeois society in which he had
been a miserable failure, self-indulgently wallow-
ing in an excess of Wagnerian romanticism? Or
was he simply a cunning opportunist using both
rational calculation and fanaticism to achieve his
real objectives? The question is still open.

The totalitarian concept implies that the authority of the dictator is total and all-embracing. It
comes as something of a surprise to learn that
Hitler was indecisive, rarely made a clear decision, tended to procrastinate, was rather lazy,
spent much of his time on nonpolitical matters,
especially the architecture of future cities, and
avoided Berlin if he could. Decision-making often
took place at lunch, where the favored few, those
who had the right of immediate access, might be
present; it is understandable that decisions were
sometimes left to chance. Since Hitler rarely
awoke before noon and spent most evenings
watching movies, the amount of time he spent on
work must have been limited. Certainly he
appears to have had little interest in domestic
affairs after the war began in 1939. Even Hans

Lammers, the head of the Reich Chancellery, did not see Hitler after September 1944 to discuss internal problems.

For Fascism and Nazism, based on the principle of leadership, there was an inherent logic in the dictatorship of an individual. For the Soviet Union, in which about two-thirds of the sixty years since 1917 have witnessed rule by an individual, this has been more difficult to justify. The modern prince in a communist system has not been the political party, the "myth prince," as Gramsci argued would be the case, but a real person.[65] Neither Marxist theory nor Leninist concept of the party can satisfactorily explain away the striking irony of the cult of personality in communist systems.

Stalin emerged as dictator more slowly than had Hitler and Mussolini. In the four major political organs established under Lenin, the Politburo, the Orgburo, the Central Committee, and the Secretariat, the only person who was a member of all was Stalin. His supposed mediocrity misled Trotsky, who later wrote, "Stalin's rise . . . occurred behind an impenetrable political curtain."[66] From his base in the Secretariat, Stalin was able to control the whole system, the official organs of party and state varying in importance depending on his will. His power to make decisions was not restrained by any group or individual. He replaced people at will in the provincial, regional and central organs of the party. Stalin liquidated not only his competitors for power, the Old Bolsheviks, makers of the 1917 revolution and associates of Lenin on false criminal charges of "counter-revolutionary" behavior including murder, espionage or sabotage. He also ruthlessly eliminated almost all those who he himself had brought into power and whom he would later accuse of "carelessness, complacency, self-satisfaction, overweening self-confident, swell-headedness and bragging."

Stalin's rise to power had been accomplished by extraordinary political skill in the formation of alliances, flexibility in changing policies at will, and manipulation of organizations and party organs to obtain support.[67] To this was added the good fortune of being able to maintain the ban on factions in the party and to label all opponents as "factionalists." He profited by the support of the growing bureaucracy and the careerists who attached themselves to him and were rewarded, at least temporarily, with privileges and special status. He made use of the large numbers of new entrants into the party which by 1928 amounted to over 1 million and constituted a different social composition than the founders of the party. Stalin was always able to persuade the party that he was the practical activist eager to avoid the divisiveness produced by his former rivals.

Under Stalin after the early state of his control there really was no ruling party except as an instrument in his hands.[68] All the voting members except one of the 1923 Politburo had been ousted by 1931. About 60 percent of the delegates to the party congress in 1934 were murdered as were 70 percent of the members and candidate members of the Central Committee in successive purges. Only 2 percent of those attending the seventeenth Congress in 1934 were present at the eighteenth in 1939. The Politburo rarely met, apparently never between 1949, when one of its members, Voznesensky, was shot, and Stalin's death in 1953. Indeed in 1952 at the nineteenth Congress the Politburo was abolished and replaced by the Central Committee Presidium. The Central Committee, supposed to meet every four months, was not convened. Until 1925 the party Congress met annually in accordance with party rules. Between 1926 and 1934 only three congresses were held, and from 1939 to 1952 none were held though a rule had been adopted in 1934 that one meet at least every three years. Under Lenin in six years there were six party Congresses, five Conferences, and sixty-nine meetings of the Central Committee. Between 1934 and 1953 there were only three Congresses, one Conference, and twenty-three meetings of the Central Committee, mostly before the war. Khrushchev sadly remembered that "Stalin rarely bothered to ask the opinion of Politburo members about a given measure."[69] Stalin ruled through his Secretariat and, later, through the "Special Sector" of the Central Committee apparatus.[70] Party secretaries were not elected as the principles of democratic centralism required, but were appointed from above.

During World War II the Politburo and the Central Committee were superseded by the Council of Ministers and other bodies after Stalin became Prime Minister and Commander-in-Chief in 1941. Many of the personnel functions of the party were performed by Stalin's aides or by the secret police. Towards the end of Stalin's rule some special sections of the department of the Central Committee of the party were responsible not to the Committee but to the secret police.[71]

• Stalin maintained power not only by terror but also by skillfully playing on the weakness and vanity of people, by giving overlapping jurisdictions to his subordinates, by arguing the need for sacrifice for the sake of the revolution, and by stressing controls against "enemies of the people," kulaks, "homeless cosmopolitans" and counterrevolutionaries, and by encouraging his own cult. He involved millions, including almost the entire party and governmental apparatus, in his crimes, which cannot be justified by reference to revolutionary needs and which are inexplicable except in terms of his own lust for power or his cruelty. The cruelty had been displayed at an early stage in his letter of May 1918 urging the ruthless burning of villages to teach their inhabitants not to raid trains.[72] It was still in evidence at the end of his life when he imprisoned the wives of close associates such as Kalinin, Molotov and Poskrebyshchev, his own secretary. During the Leningrad case between 1949 and 1951, in which thousands were arrested for allegedly conspiring to establish an independent Russian Communist party and to make Leningrad the capital of a Russian republic, Stalin eliminated Vosnesensky, his second in command, first deputy chairman of the Council of Ministers and a member of the Politburo. In 1952 General Vlasik, head of Stalin's own personal bodyguard, was arrested. The January 1953 so-called "doctors' plot" was ominous in its implication since six of the nine doctors accused of committing medical murders on the orders of United States intelligence were Jews. Only two weeks before Stalin's death Ivan Maisky, former Ambassador to Britain, was arrested at the age of sixty-nine.

The tragic Bukharin, a few years before his execution, called Stalin "a small-minded malicious man—no, not a man but a devil—who resented anyone more competent than himself." Part of the reason for the show trials of the 1930s was to cover up his appalling mistakes. Everyone was obliged to proclaim his devotion to him; he had monuments built to himself and cities and factories named after him. History was falsified to allow him to become the real maker of the 1917 revolution, with a little assistance from Lenin. The dictator became omniscient as his genius extended to music and linguistics as well as to philosophy, ethics, history, culture, social science, and economic planning. In his official biography, edited by himself, Stalin modestly appears as a "genius, without the slightest hint of vanity, pride or self conceit," the incomparable master of the Marxist dialectical method, the teacher of the masses, the brilliant strategist of the proletarian revolution.

But Stalin in fact imperiled the safety of the country by his slaughter of the officer corps. He murdered three of the country's five marshals, leaving only the two political marshals, 14 of 16 army commanders, all the eight admirals, 60 of the 67 corps commanders, 136 of the 199 divisional commanders, 221 of the 397 brigade commanders, and most of the political commissars attached to military units.

At all times from the Revolution until the present the military has been subordinated to the political rulers. The potential unreliability of the Red Army, which was obliged to accept some 50,000 officers and 200,000 noncommissioned officers of the Tsarist army to help fight the civil war after 1917, led to the creation of political commissars who shared authority with the military commander and were responsible for propaganda. After the victory of the Red Army in 1921 the role of the commanders and their ability to take independent decisions was increased until the purges of the 1930s and the restoration of a more coequal role for the commissars in 1937. Throughout World War II Stalin changed the relative power relationship between the two groups of leaders.

Political control over the military has been maintained from the Stalinist era by a variety of methods: by attempting to ensure that all officers were party members and thus subject to discipline, by political indoctrination by a party organ, the Main Political Administration of the armed forces, by having the territorial party organs check on the military units in their jurdisdiction, by the military council at the regional level, by the promotion of politically reliable officers and the employment of political generals, by the use of secret police in the armed forces, and by material rewards.[73] If the influence of the military has fluctuated in different periods, depending on political circumstances and personnel, it has not yet constituted any real challenge to the dominant position of the political rulers.

Stalin's role extended beyond the Soviet Union. From the formation of the Comintern, it was understood that foreign communist parties must defend the Soviet Union, which could intervene in their internal affairs. In the 1930s Stalin appointed and purged the leadership of the Eastern European parties and even dissolved the Polish communist party to assuage Hitler. As the war ended, Stalin presided over the creation of communist-dominated systems in Eastern Europe. He managed to control them by a variety of methods including ordering purges of those leaders who had not spent the war in Moscow. The political systems of the satellites imitated the Soviet Union, which laid down policy guidelines as well as incorporating the countries in its economic embrace.

Since the death of Stalin, the Soviet Union has alternated between a tendency to dictatorial personal power and oligarchic collective decision-making.[74] Though the latter seems to have been the norm for certain periods under both Khruschchev and Brezhnev, the system has always reverted to one in which the individual leader has asserted his dominant position.

5
Total Control

The distinctiveness of totalitarianism, as the word suggests, is total control over the lives and actions of citizens. Control can be regarded either as restrictive of, or as compelling to, action. From the restrictive point of view, as both Lenin and Gentile declared, there were no limits to state action, and consequently, rulers could apply any restraints against their population. Nothing was purely private: normal behavior and daily life could be subordinated to the values of the regime. Total control was necessary if the prevailing ideology was to be implemented. The totalitarian state was dominated not simply by police but by an intellectual idea.[75] Control meant the regulation not only of overt action but also of suspected intention to act. The consequence of this attitude, as Arendt argued, was that totalitarian government destroyed private as well as public life.[76] Even worse than regulation and prevention of action, however, was the criminal involvement of large numbers of citizens in the activities of the regime aimed at implementing its basic ideas.[77]

All three systems stressed the need for solidarity. For the Soviet Union the solidarity was supposedly international in character, extending to the working class everywhere. In reality it was achieved at the expense of the destruction of the working class as political force, the elimination of free trade unions and the end of internal democracy within the party. For Fascism and National Socialism, all classes and groups of people in the nation would work together to restore the grandeur of Italy or to fulfill the destiny of Germany, thus ending internal class conflict or social disorder. Such systems would supersede those based on liberal democracy which was negative and anarchic in nature, or on religious and social traditions in which aristocratic privileges prevailed. They would no longer be the expression of particular interests. In this organic view of the nation characterized by discipline and obedience there was an identity of interests between workers and employers. It is not coincidental that Mussolini in 1914 named his new paper, *Il Popolo d'Italia*. Nor that Hitler in his first speech as Chancellor in 1933 appealed to workers and farmers for national unity. The appeal was made more meaningful by the process of *Gleichschaltung,* the coordination and control of all organizations, whose autonomy was thus ended.

The economy, the cultural elite, the church, the bureaucracy, the military, all served the system. Only the ambitions of other Nazi leaders blocked the attempt by the Minister of the Interior to centralize control of the Gleichschaltung process which concerned the police and the military as well as social and economic affairs.

The police came under this controlling process not only by Nazi leaders heading the different branches of the police organizations but also by Himmler's joint incumbency as Chief of the German Police and as Reichsführer SS in June 1936. The police received political and ideological training by the Race and Settlement Office of the SS which was responsible for disseminating racial doctrines, enforcing the SS marriage law and for arresting "inferior persons" in the countries occupied during the war. The police were expected to become models of correct Nazi behavior and to become bearers of the political will of National Socialism. The regular police was also obliged to cooperate with the Gestapo in combatting "political crimes," to participate in enforcing measures against Jews and workers, and to serve in the military forces under the supreme command of the SS.[78]

The military hierarchy was in a more ambiguous position in the early years. Military values formed a significant element of German political culture, the result of inculcation in youth camps, the prominence of veterans in governmental positions, the impact of historical memories, and the special status and privileged position of the Officer Corps. In January 1933 General von Hammerstein, the Commander in Chief, protested against the appointment of Hitler as Chancellor. Among the German Generals only one, Reichenau, appeared to be a Nazi when Hitler took power. But the army had played its part in allowing Hitler's accession to power. In particular General von Schleicher had induced President Hindenburg to appoint Hitler as Chancellor.

In the Weimar regime the army leaders had claimed a status "above politics." They quickly made a pact with the Nazis to preserve their position. Hitler's agreement with the Reichswehr on January 30, 1933 was that the army would keep out of politics and support the regime in return for being protected against the SA, maintaining its honored place in German society, regaining some of its former privileges and obtaining assurances of rapid rearmanent. On March 21, 1933 Hitler staged "The Day of Potsdam" to link his regime to past traditions, including the glories of the Prussian Army. He ended the jurisdiction of the civil courts over the armed forces and spoke of the latter as "the sole bearer of arms in the nation." But, if the SA was purged in 1934 partly on its insistence, the military lost any possibility of independent action in 1938 with the ignominious fall of Generals Blomberg and von Fritsch. The officer corps was constrained from disobedience by the oath of "unconditional obedience to Adolf Hitler" taken when Hitler combined the offices of Chancellor and President on the death of Hindenburg and became Commander in Chief of the armed forces in August 1934. It was humiliated, brought under the control of Hitler and became an accessory in the brutalities of the regime. The military complied in the killing of Soviet prisoners of war and provided logistical support to the Einsatzgruppen, the special task forces who killed Jews and Poles in Eastern Europe. Its attempts to restrain Hitler in the invasions of the Rhineland, Austria, Czechoslovakia and Poland were all frustrated, and the generals were excluded from his intimate entourage. Hitler complained on September 24, 1941 that the General Staff had always been a hindrance in doing what he thought necessary. The final humiliation came on July 29, 1944, nine days after the unsuccessful assassination attempt on Hitler, with the order that "Every General Staff Officer must be a National Socialist Officer-leader."[79] No member of the General Staff resigned or resisted. Its power as a state within the state was ended.

The state itself would be the living organism of the people, leading them to the highest freedom. The solidarity and union of purpose, achieved by a mixture of force and indoctrination, and including brainwashing and biological breeding (menschenenzüchtung), would lead to a new form of social relationships and a new individual. For the middle class this implied that their welfare was equated with that of the nation as a whole rather than the result of assertion of private interest. Class conflict was supposed to be overcome by class reconciliation, though in practice the result was subordination of the working class. For class warfare would be substituted warfare between nations or races. People were to be organically structured in professions, organized on hierarchical lines, though the organizations in fact had little effective power. But if in theory the Nazi objective was, as Schoenbaum suggests,[80] the creation of a psychologically classless society, in reality it was a society of which the unfit, physical and political, could not be members and were to be eliminated. Both Nazism and Fascism would create a new man, vital, virile, and strong, who would be loyal to the regime. The most extreme embodiment of the new man was the SS paragon

adhering to the motto "Meine Ehre heisst Treue"
(My honor is loyalty) and whose highest priority
was to "be honest, decent, loyal and comradely to
members of our own blood and to nobody else."
Such behavior would lead to a race of rulers, a
breed of viceroys, strong in spirit and in body. The
Fascist revolution would be fulfilled only when
Italy was populated by Fascist citizens.[81]

National unity would be enhanced by the participation and mobilization of the masses. The participation in Germany was partly implemented
through referenda and plebiscites providing 99.9
percent approval, and in the other countries by
periodic elections which produced the same result.
But the mobilization meant not that the population would be brought into the policy-making process, but that it would be organized and
manipulated to carry out the goals of the regimes.
In the Nazi regime the manipulation embraced the
creation of a national mystique through rites, festivals, myths, and symbols, which were to give
concrete expression to the general will of the community. A variety of devices—holy flames, theatre, gymnastics, choirs, flags, songs, national
monuments—transformed political action into
drama. All normally nonpolitical activities were
exploited to aid in the creation of the Nazi political
style and to gain support for Nazi political objectives. Sport was essential for spiritual and ideological education and would develop the strength for
world conquest. A secular religion was being
created in which there would be "no spectators,
only actors."[82] Formal religion was to be replaced
by the heroic figures and places of the regime. If

Horst Wessel became the glorified martyr for the Nazis, Lenin became the saint of the Communist party. The place where the former was murdered, and the square where the latter lies embalmed both became holy shrines. The revolutionary year, in all three systems, became the equivalent of the Day of Judgment and the start of the periodization of history.[83]

The differences in the mobilization processes illustrate the historical specificities of the regimes and the cultural contexts in which they existed, and resulted from the varied nature and number of tasks to be performed. The Nazi regime, a sophisticated centralized system, tended to concentrate on the mass media and required a high quality of propaganda for mass activities. Goebbels was the Minister for Propaganda *and* Enlightenment. He was, as Trevor-Roper has recently argued, the first person to realize the full potentialities of the mass media for political purposes in a dynamic totalitarian state.[84] Using the technique of the big lie, Goebbels insisted that propaganda must appeal to the emotions rather than to reason and that its success depended on repetition. The Soviet Union, at a lower industrial and cultural level, stressed to a greater degree oral agitation at the personal level. Some of the major purposes of mobilization varied: in the Soviet Union work and discipline were stressed, while in Germany racial purity and struggle were emphasized. Inevitably there were different degrees of general acceptance of the policies:[85] the abolition of unemployment and the strengthening of Germany through rearmament were more popular than were the Soviet policies which called for sacrifices in the interest of industrial productivity. The call for productivity and the need to recover from the Civil War and the famine, led to an emphasis on socialist competition, which in effect meant the encouraging the speeding up of production, exemplified to an extreme degree by Stakhanovism after 1935.

The chief instrument of mobilization was the party, either directly through its own hierarchical organization or indirectly, through its control of associated groups such as trade unions, youth, cultural, sport and professional groups, the groups called "transmission belts" by Lenin because they were used by the party to communicate with the masses and to ensure execution of its policy. The result was considerable popular support for Stalinism. The imposed popular culture may have been especially attractive to the uncultured population who were leaving rural for urban areas. A possible explanation for the acceptance by many of the validity of the charges of sabotage and wrecking was the illiteracy of the country which, in addition to religious traditions, made charges of "heresy" familiar. As late as 1927 only seven percent of all party members had received any secondary education. The cult of Stalin himself grew into a religious phenomena, "a peculiar Soviet form of worship" as Medvedev expressed it.[86] In a more mundane fashion many profited from the increase in official jobs and privileges brought by the growth of state activity. Even the purges were agreeable to workers who approved the downfall of party and state officials.

The German people was to be mobilized to understand the crisis it faced and to be capable of dealing with internal and external enemies. The Nazi party, which by 1943 had reached a membership of almost 2 million, propagated the word of the Führer and was expected to exemplify desirable behavior such as volunteering for action, attending meetings, and espousing anti-Semitic attitudes. The party organization, with its base in the residential block, was connected with the whole population. To this were related the affiliated organizations such as the German Labor Front, the NS-People's Welfare, and party formations such as the SA and Hitler Youth. Only the SS, an elite corps, was outside the control of the party.

Labor organizations were an especially important mechanism for participation of the whole community which would appreciate the dignity of labor. The German Labor Front (D.A.F.), established in May 1933 immediately after the free trade union movement was ended and collective bargaining was abolished and made an official organ in October 1934, had as its purported objective the creation of "a real community of the people in life and work." This would include employers as well as employees and would assist the economy by its participation in social insurance, vocational training and publication of trade journals. Led by Robert Ley, party boss from Cologne, the Nazis were able to dominate the DAF which was organized in lines similar to the party.

The Labor Front through its Strength Through Joy (K.d.F.) organ successfully sponsored cheap holidays and entertainment. Through the K.d.F. leisure was to be used for propaganda purposes, all members of the community were to be brought

together, and Germans could become familiar
with different sections of their country so that
regional differences could be overcome.[87] By their
attempt to form a united community under Nazi
auspices both the parent D.A.F. and the offspring
K.d.F. tried to obliterate memories of the old trade
unions and organizations. Traditional holidays
such as May Day were converted to Nazi purposes,
as were celebrations connected with birth, marriage, and death, and Sunday morning celebrations. Worker's competitions for decorations
helped create harmonious factory relations. The
mobilization process also made use of social welfare programs or the provision of benefits, not
only through the NS-People's Welfare organization, but also through the annual Winter Help col-
lection, and assistance and welfare to families of
soldiers, especially in times of distress.

The youth of the country were socialized
through a series of organizations in which membership was compulsory for all youth between the
ages of ten and eighteen after December 1936
(though it was not implemented for three years
and not fully applicable until September 1941)
from the Jungvolk and Jungmädelbund to the
Hitler Youth and the Federation of German Girls.
By 1938 the total membership had already
reached 8.75 million. Alternative youth groups—
the middle class Bundische Jugend as well as the
Protestant, Catholic and Socialist leagues—were
all eliminated. Yet it is arguable that the Hitler
Youth (HJ) movement could fully control German
youth. Problems arose because of the shortage of
competent leaders, poor training methods, concentration on marches and demonstrations, interfer-

ence with normal school work, and the coarseness of its dissemination of ideology.[88] The vulgarity of many of the HJ leaders repelled Catholics in particular. Its main conception of education was sport and physical prowess which would in fact fulfill the objectives stated by Hitler in September 1935 that "the German youth of the future must be slim and slender, swift as the greyhound, tough as leather, and hard as Krupp steel."[89] It sought both to indoctrinate youth, especially in the subjects of German racial superiority and anti-Semitism, and to control the moral and social behavior of its members including the prevention of delinquency and criminality. But to obtain compliance the HJ launched campaigns for compulsory attendance, laid down threats of punishments graded in hierarchical fashion, and supervised its members by the Patrol Service, its internal police.

There was an inevitable difference of opinion between the HJ and the teaching profession in general which refused to accept the adage of the aging Reich Youth Leader, Baldur von Schirach, that "youth is always right" and which was coerced into undertaking clerical and administrative work for the party.[90] The teachers were aware of a serious decline in the levels of academic achievement. Higher education was seriously restricted. The academic year was shortened from thirty to twenty weeks a year, and the number of students in both universities and technical institutes decreased almost 50 percent between 1933 and 1939.

There was relatively little coercion on teachers to belong to the NS Dozentenbund, and the academic profession continued to recruit from its own

ranks. Yet the educational establishment bears
responsibility for approving, or passively acquies-
ing in, Nazi concepts or activities such as indoctrination of anti-Semitism, Aryan science, book
burnings, the abandonment of scientific objectiv-
ity and outbreaks of violence. Though Hannah
Arendt tried to defend her former teacher Martin
Heidegger at the celebration of his eightieth birth-
day, the speech of the famous philosopher on his
inaugural as rector of Freiburg University in May
1933 when he talked of the three services—labor,
military, and knowledge—that German students
could provide the state, and his later pledge of
unconditional loyalty to "the savior of our nation"
are poignant examples of the depths to which German academics had fallen. Heidegger had forgot-
ten the aphorism of Heine a century earlier: after
the burning of the books will come the burning of
men.

Similar youth groups were formed in Italy. The
attempt to use the educational system for propaganda was not wholly successful, especially in the
south and particularly at the university level, for
both teachers and students resisted indoctrination. More important for this purpose were the
youth organizations, the Opera Nazionale Balilla
and its successor the GIL. Perhaps most important of all was the Dopolavoro, the main and most
active organization through which the regime
influenced the leisure of the urban population.
Sports and culture were both used for political purposes. But censorship of the theatre and films was
haphazard and often dependent on Mussolini's
whims.[91] Some diversity of the press remained

until the censorship of the Press Office and the Ministry of Popular Culture in the mid-1930s. Control was never as strong or effective as in Germany; there was room for independence in literature and art. But Mussolini tried to mobilize the energies of the Italians and integrate them into the regime.[92]

In the Soviet Union, mobilization was to a large degree based on terror, but direct and indirect forms of social control were always widely employed. The educational process, the continual rewriting of history and censorship served this objective. Even the purges, with their trials and confessions, were used for educating the people about the current enemies and for gaining support for the leadership who were eliminating those enemies. Lenin had distinguished between agitation that aimed at an emotional impact on a mass audience and propaganda that aimed at a more politically literate audience. But both were as much concerned with practical problems as they were with strictly ideological matters, which in any event are more difficult to comprehend.[93] At both the residential and work place levels, the party has used agitators, perhaps 3.50 million, who try to persuade people by example, exhortation, rewards and sanctions, to satisfy the economic goals of the regime. Persuasion into the desirable values has been attempted by the concept of "socialist realism" that has dominated Soviet culture, by the educational curriculum which has included courses in communist doctrine, and by the example of honors given to outstanding workers, the "Heroes of Soviet Labor."

The very model of the socialist hero as portrayed
in literature changed from a practical individual
contributing to the welfare of society to one acting
under the guidance of Stalin in a hierarchical system.[94] Political education, including the adult education system, has been more concerned with
ideological indoctrination, though the surfeit of
lectures and conferences has taken its toll. More
recently, the polit-informator, a specialist on a
particular topic, has been used. Indoctrination
has also been indirect, through the manipulation
of family evenings, folk dancing, amateur drama,
and the use of public holidays and festivals. Youth
organizations—the Little Octobrists, Young Pio-
neers, and Komsomols—have been used as in the
other two countries. Alternative sources of ethics
and values such as religion were subject to attack
by the educational process, teaching of materialist
philosophy, party and youth activism and by the
Union of Godless Zealots founded in 1925. Even
the Orthodox Church reached accomodation with
the regime with the September 1943 agreement by
which Stalin, in recognition of the loyalty of the
Church and aware of the persistence of religious
feeling, allowed the Church to reestablish a central organization and to elect a Patriarch.

6
Total Scope and Economics

It has sometimes been argued that the apparatus of a totalitarian state embraces a total monopoly over the economy, politics, police, unions, culture, the legislature, the military, information media and educational process.[95] However, in practice the three regimes did not bear out the principle of total control of economic activity. If there was a consistency about the economic controls, though wide variations in policy, in the Soviet Union, there was no such consistency in Italy and Germany.[96]

In Germany, control of labor was introduced gradually: freedom of movement was limited in 1934 in order to prevent migration to towns, and labor passes were instituted in 1935. In the latter year national labor service for six months before two years service in the army was made compulsory so that all would contribute to the community. In 1934 Social Honor Courts were established

63

to punish employers who misused their authority
or violated their social duties, and employees who
engaged in willful and malicious agitation or who
disturbed the community spirit. Complete control
of movement was assumed in 1938-39 because of
the need to construct border fortifications. Foreign
workers were expelled. Labor was controlled
through "work-books" and by special passports
for workers who thus could not voluntarily change
jobs. It was the rearmament program that in 1936
had already created shortages of raw materials
and labor, and the increased importance of the
chemical industry relative to heavy industry generally, that accounts for changes in economic relationships and more stringent controls.[97] From
1938 all employers needed the consent of labor
exchange to hire workers. State intervention
would be necessary, Hitler said, "only if people
should fail to act in the interests of the nation."[98]
This meant the destruction of the free trade union
movement and the elimination of labor as an
organized political force. The short working day
could be permitted, not out of any ideological conviction but to ensure full employment. In industrial plants the party members in the plant were
often the real leaders of the enterprise. Workers
"suspected of an attitude hostile to the state" could
be arbitrarily dismissed. The shortage of labor led
in 1938 and 1939 to maximum wage levels being
imposed on certain branches of industry and to
other forms of labor controls. Immediately following the outbreak of war in 1939, the Trustees of
Labor, who had been appointed under the
National Labor Law to maintain industrial peace

and to decide on wage scales as well as other conditions of work, were empowered to fix maximum wages and to regulate working conditions in all branches of industry. But although wages were frozen in October 1939, bonus rates for some work were allowed. In general German industry was not fully mobilized, and planning and total control of the economy—resources, wage, and price controls—were achieved only during the war. It is still an open question at what moment the German economy became totally oriented toward a war policy. In a perceptive essay[99] Sidney Ratner has analyzed the different schools of thought on the subject. One view argues that preparation for war had dominated economic policy from the beginning of the Nazi regime and that all resources were mobilized for this end. The other analysis suggests that full mobilization did not occur until the middle of the war. A cautious and careful assessment has been made by Berenice Carroll[100] drawing evidence from the percentage of the gross national product devoted to military expenditure, the percentage of government expenditure devoted to military purposes and the relative proportions of total investment for military and civilian purposes. This assessment suggests that Germany began to move in the direction of a war economy in 1934 and became dominated in certain key aspects by armaments in 1936. A war economy did not really exist until 1938 and a full total war economy not until 1942. Intense rivalries between organizations and people prevented any centralized control over the process until the appointment of Fritz Todt as Minister of Muni-

tions in 1940 led to a major effort to provide some
central direction to the war effort. The centralization and total control over armaments and war
production were enhanced when Albert Speer succeeded Todt on his death in 1942. In a recent
work[101] T. W. Mason has argued that their concern
for popular support prevented the Nazis, in spite of
their policy of rapid militarization, from full economic mobilization which would have required
major sacrifices in peacetime.

Some of the regulations of industry and handicrafts was performed by cartels and various business associations. Nevertheless in 1934 the
Minister for Economic Affairs also became the
leader of the Organization of Handicrafts, Industry and Trade which became a part of the Labor
Front by the Leipzig Agreement of March 1935.
Industry was thus subject to the party. There was
similar control over agriculture. Since the farm
population was supposed to be preserved as the
"source of blood of the German people" a law of
September 1933 attempted to preserve economic
farms not larger than 125 hectares (309 acres). The
National Food Estate was set up in 1933 to com-
bine all agricultural activities from the farm to the
ultimate consumer, but it was headed by the
National Farm Leader who also became Minister
of Agriculture and who was appointed by Hitler
not by the farm organizations.

In Italy the totalitarian facade was not a true
image of reality, in that much economic activity
was not publicly controlled. The October 1925 Pact
of Vidoni Palace set up two monopolies of employers and workers, each to represent its side in collec-

tive bargaining. The right to strike was virtually ended, the workers' shop councils abolished and the workers' organization subjected to control. The 1926 Rocco law ended Italy's free labor movement which was replaced by fascist union organizations and syndicates. But industry, through the General Confederation of Italian Industry, was represented in the Grand Council and was often strong enough to resist the demands of government.[102] The state leaned to the side of industry. Where the state intervened it was to save industry, as in 1933, when the Institute of Industrial Reorganization (IRI) was set up to aid bankrupt concerns. The Italian state was termed "corporative" in 1926 but in fact no corporations existed until 1934. Private enterprise existed alongside the public enterprises in fields such as shipping, mining, oil and production of war materials. Not until the Ethiopian War in 1936 were key industries nationalized.

The regime reduced the level of real industrial wages because of the economic depression. In addition, it smashed the labor organizations and imposed restrictions on internal migration by regulating changes in residence, requiring a job passport of all workers, and finally in 1939 governing the hiring and placement of workers.[103] The reasons given for regulation were to tie the peasantry to the soil, to reach autarky, and to check the growth of cities. But equally practical reasons were the burden of housing programs and the political utility of controlling the population. Though industry in general was not nationalized, the state was concerned with the location of and investment in new plants or extensions and with the establishment of public works in order to reduce unemployment.

But the economic policies not only fostered restrictive industrial and trade monopolies but also led to production yielding low returns and modernization being limited. Economically, the regime never solved its problems. In 1922 there were 407,000 unemployed; in 1935, when publication of unemployment statistics was suspended, there were 765,000. In the South there was little real reform in the holding and use of land: between 1928 and 1938 per capita income in the South fell 2 percent while it increased 4.4 percent in the North. The growth of national income as a whole was retarded. Wage cuts had to be compensated for by family allowances, Christmas bonuses, and in 1941 an earnings equalization fund. The regime produced industrial cartels, public works programs, a short work week, and the subjugation of labor.

However it does not follow that the German and Italian regimes should be seen as capitalist in nature, or as the last stage of monopoly capitalism that Marxist analysis has suggested. In view of the fact that Italy in 1922 was not industrially mature, such analysis appears inadequate anyway. To argue, as Franz Neumann did,[104] that "profits and more profits are the motive power" of Nazism, does not explain the complexity of the regime. Nor does the thesis that it was plebian anticapitalism that was the major feature differentiating twentieth century conservative and semiparliamentary regimes.[105] It is true that private business benefited in the two regimes, that cartelization occurred, and that business interests were served by the ending of class struggle. But private control of industry and the making of profits were incidental to Hitler's objectives. For tactical reasons, the gaining of electoral support, he cultivated the middle class, explaining, for example in 1928, that the party program that called for the expropriation of land without compensation really meant only the land owned by Jewish property speculation companies.[106] In 1932 he appointed Walter Funk, who was trusted by industrialists, to be his liaison with business. In power his objectives—the elimination of Jews, the thrust for Lebensraum—and his methods, including coercion and paramilitary organizations, were not those of business, as the disputes over the nature of the larger German area and the transfer of foreign workers to Germany showed.

Planning in the early stage of the Nazi regime was aimed at rescuing agriculture and eliminating unemployment largely through the establishment of public works, but the economy was soon transformed to serve the overriding objective of rearmament and military readiness. This meant the development of an armaments economy and the building of the necessary infrastructure such as highways, barracks and relocated industrial plants, and compulsory labor service.[107] It also implied a campaign for autarky and a search for alternative commodities in which Germany was deficient. The economy, wrote Goering in February 1937, had to conform "with the uniform will of the supreme leadership as with a supreme funda-

mental law." This logically entailed a closed as
well as a controlled economy with governmental
powers extending to foreign trade and exchanges,
raw materials, capital and credits, prices, wages
and manpower.

More than one writer has pointed out that the
original Fascist and Nazi Programs were anticapitalist as well as nationalist. In 1920 the Nazis proposed the abolition of unearned income and
opposed "rapacious" capitalism. The Italian Fascists in 1919, under pressure from the movement's
revolutionary syndicalist wing, proposed a capital
levy, a tax on war profits, minimum wage rates,
and workers' participation in management.[108]
Fascism was neither counter-revolutionary nor a
tool of big business. But its stress on national
unity as well as the difficult economic problems
that existed meant suppression of working class
demands, the prohibition of strikes, the destruction of socialist agrarian organizations, and the
stopping of class conflict on behalf of society as a
whole. For the Fascists economic health and military strength were more likely to be satisfied by
big business than by small units.

In the Nazi and Fascist systems large industry
may have benefited from but did not direct policy.
On the whole big business did not support Hitler in
his rise to power, except for political insurance; his
industrial support came from small and medium
sized businesses.[109] It was of little significance to
the rulers whether an enterprise was in private
hands or under state control. The Commonwealth
had priority over private profit (Gemeinnutz gehr
vor Eigennutz). Some of the public undertakings

in roadmaking, land improvement, rail and waterways, through which unemployment was to be reduced were administered by government directly while others were carried out by private firms on the basis of government standards and conditions.[110] For the same reason subsidies were given to private building operations and rebates of taxation were provided for renovation of industrial equipment. The economic effects of Hitler's political activities, or foreign policy, were of secondary significance to him.

Though the system allowed the making of private profit, capitalism in the traditional sense of a free market of supply and demand was subordinated to the development of a military economy in which the government decided on investment, production, distribution and consumption. By a statute of June 1939 the Reichsbank was made directly responsible to the Führer and Chancellor. Already in December 1934 the government had obtained jurisdiction over all nongovernmental credit institutions and control over banks which were still permitted to be privately owned. The tax laws were interpreted and tax policy formulated to achieve Nazi policies or implement principles such as stimulating employment, encouraging the growth of population, facilitating rearmament or increasing the degree of self-sufficiency.[111] Political goals incompatible in nature, such as full employment, price stability, rearmament, industrial recovery, expansion of exports, and autarky, dominated economic policy.[112] The regime fulfilled some promises in ending unemployment, improving working conditions, and taking care of leisure activities. But others, such as increase in agricultural prices, could not be fulfilled because of the fear of inflation. The rapid increase in rearmament helped produced a labor shortage, thus resulting in both higher wages in industry and in the migration from the land that the Nazis had pledged to stop.

The creation of the Soviet Union illustrated the priority of politics over economics. Leninist tactics contradicted Marx's view that the making of a socialist revolution was linked to the ripeness of the capitalist productive forces. Instead, using Marxian terminology, the superstructure would alter the economic substructure and social relationships and not the reverse. In 1926 Stalin declared that "the main task of the proletarian revolution consists in seizing power in order to build up a new Socialist economy."

The Stalinist period exemplified the principle of total control over the economy to a greater degree than did the Nazi and Fascist systems. "War Communism" from 1917 to 1921 led to the nationalization of land, forced grain requisitions from the peasants, and the creation of agricultural communes. With the New Economic Policy of 1921-28 the state removed many restrictions on the peasants and allowed trade and small industry to operate in private hands. But for Stalin, ideology required that the country be industrialized and the peasantry subordinated to the proletariat. A mixture of motives led Russia to want to catch up with the capitalist West. For this purpose the state, for Stalin, had to exercise complete control over economic life. Starting in 1928 the regime eliminated almost all individual ownership of land, created collective and state farms, and initiated the process of rapid industrialization. The collectivization of agriculture was supposedly necessary to provide capital needed to import machinery and foreign technical assistance, as well as to supply sufficient food for the increasing urban population.

The pace and direction of industrialization, the implementation of collectivization, and the extermination of the kulaks was determined by Stalin. The revolution was imposed "from above on the initiative of the state" at tremendous cost and loss of life. The autonomy of the trade unions virtually ended in 1930 when they became agents of the state, the right to strike was taken away, and workers were subjected to strict discipline through a strong labor code. Labor passports limited choice of work. Work norms, on which wages depended, were established. Managers of enterprises assumed authority for the expansion of production. Millions of people were sent to work in the labor camps. By 1936, Stalin claimed, there were only two groups in the Soviet Union, working peasants and workers, and the intelligentsia. But the state, far from withering away as Marxist theory projected, had become stronger than ever. To explain this Stalin formulated his famous contradictory or, as he preferred it, dialectical statement of June 1930 that "we are for the withering away of the state. And at the same time we stand for the strengthening of the dictatorship of the proletariat, representing the strongest and most powerful authority of all existing state authorities up to the present time."

7

A Monolithic Entity?

Embedded in the concept of totalitarianism, perhaps more implicitly than explicitly, is the assumption of a monolithic entity with clarity both in jurisdiction and decision making. But the experience of the regimes suggests that such an assumption is not wholly justified. The supposed monolithic entities suffered power struggles within the ruling group, diffusion of decision making, and a complex, often unclear, relationship between party and state.

Less is known about Soviet affairs in this regard than about the other two countries, but even there practice seems to have differed from theory. The Soviet Union could be characterized as a monolithic system, with its centralization of party organization and loss of autonomy by local parties, minimization of the power of the Red Army through purges, through isolation of its leaders from the party organization, and through the allocation of responsibility for ideological indoctrination and control to political commissars or political officers, withdrawal of any real independence in important decision making from the constituent republics of the country, neglect and minimization of the Soviets, and elimination of the party leadership by Stalin.[113] Yet in the Soviet Union there were always divisions between those concerned with technical and those with verbal matters, between industrial and agricultural experts, and between geographical areas and nationalities. The administration, theoretically hierarchical in nature, was in reality full of mutual suspicion and was often bypassed. A number of central agencies such as the Ministry of Finance, the Ministry of State Control and the State Planning Commission (Gosplan), all subordinate to Stalin and his personal staff, were used to check on the administration and to prevent the rise of a bureaucratic esprit. Stalin encouraged the rivalry between his subordinates to prevent any combination against him. Inner conflicts after Stalin's death led to the postponement of some decisions like the virgin soil issue in 1954. An intense, violent, and divisive power struggle occurred over the Berlin crisis of 1961.[114] The Cuban missile crisis brought Khrushchev down.

Divisions existed from the beginning within the Italian Fascist movement with its mixture of revolutionary syndicalists, futurists, nationalists, and military desperadoes, the squadristi. The goals of the latter group—an elitist organization, local power for the ras, a military spirit to be imposed on all—were not those of the syndicalists, who wanted class cooperation and national solidarity. In the early years Mussolini, who could not control the provincial squadre which had developed spontaneously, turned the movement into a party, the Partito Nazionale Fascista.

The party itself experienced a series of internal crises—on local matters, on policy, on the role of the militia, on party organization, and on differences between the northern and southern branches.[115] There were differences between the nationalists like Federzoni and the more extreme Fascists like Farinacci, between the early and late Fascists, between the militia and the squads. In 1924 Rocca lost his fight for technical councils against the ras. Usually more extreme, the ras fought against the revisionists, who were willing to accept an authoritarian system with limited pluralism.[116] There were disagreements between the syndicalists led by Rossoni, wanting to retain separate workers' and employers' organizations and to concentrate on labor problems, and the corporativists, wanting an integrated working community and concerned primarily with production. The influence of the party and the quality of its leadership varied through the country.

Mussolini maintained control by mediating among the rival forces and by subordinating the party to the state after 1926. He disagreed with some of his close associates: Federzoni, who was an authoritarian nationalist, Rocco, a corporativist, and Bocchini, a political police chief.[117] "After the revolution," remarked Mussolini, "there is always the question of the revolutionaries." He put an end to any revolutionary expecta-

tions that more radical Fascists may have had of
the creation of a new society and of a new type of
man. The syndicalist element early lost its influence. The much discussed corporations, which
were to be the cornerstone of the new society, did
not come into existence until 1934 and never really
functioned as intended, if they functioned at all.

Fascism was always constrained by the presence of the old conservative or traditional groups
and personnel. The retention of the monarchy
meant that it could be seen as an alternative, if not
a source of power, with senior officials and even
some party leaders pledging devotion to the king.
It took only a simple act of the king to legitimize
Mussolini's ouster in 1943. The army supported
the regime in return for virtual autonomy. The militia did not remain a Fascist tool; rather, it became
an adjunct of the army. The judiciary largely
remained unchanged until 1941, though it did not
oppose the regime or offer legal resistance.[118]

Mussolini soon came to terms with the Church,
allowing religious teaching in the primary
schools, increasing the salary of the clergy, and
saving the Vatican's Bank of Rome from bank-
ruptcy. But it was the Lateran Pacts of 1929 that
allowed the Church to provide an alternative set of
values. Not only was the independence of the Pap-
acy and its sovereignty in the Vatican recognized,
Catholicism accepted as the state religion, and
religious instruction imposed on the schools, but
also Catholic Action was allowed to survive and
compete with Fascist cultural and social groups.
The Church never became a focus of opposition to
the regime, but the protection of its authority

belied the possibility that Fascism could be seen as an "ethical state" in Gentile's phrase or a "total state" in Rocco's, or that there was a total identification of state and society.

The economic and social system emerged virtually unchanged from the Fascist era. The only major problem that was solved was that of the Church. The Mezzogiorno was not integrated into the rest of the country nor Southern attitudes changed.[119] The policy of population increase had little perceptible effect. There was little improvement in the standard of living of the Italian people. There were no long term reforms.[120] Economic growth was modest, though more rapid in the 1930's, the attempt at autarky failed, and the country became virtually self-sufficient in wheat only at the expense of other products.

There were similar differences among the Nazi leaders, on the degree of desirable change, on the movement as an elitist or mass organization, on the respective authority of the Gauleiters and the center, on whether the party should merge with other organizations or remain as a control instrument, on the independence of the paramilitary organizations and later of the Labor Front. There were divisions even over anti-Semitic policy between the Ministry of Economics and the SS, and between the SD and the Gestapo. A bitter conflict occurred during the war between the Party Chancellery under Bormann and the SS.

Peterson has shown that at the different political levels, national, regional, and local, there was confusion in performance of jobs, overlapping of administrative jurisdictions without coordination, personal conflict, organizational disputes, and competition both between officials of party and state, and between different party organizations and local leaders. Hitler clearly employed the classic device of divide and rule and limited the authority of subleaders to their particular spheres.[121] But his indolence and dislike for administration left a vacuum. The intrigues and divisions continued to the end, with leaders directing autonomous empires staffed by local supporters who fought off the attacks on their domain.[122]

Striking examples of this conflict were evident in propaganda and in economic policy as well as in many other areas. In propaganda, struggles were rife between Goebbels, supposedly in charge of all publications, and intruders like Goering in art, Rosenberg in literature and culture, Amann in the press, and Dietrich, the Reich press chief. In intelligence gathering there were disputes between the military Abwehr, the SS Nachrichtendienst, a Foreign Office group, a unit of the Ministry of Propaganda and the Ostministerium. In economic policy Schacht, when Minister of Economics, managed to prevail over the Nazi demand for control of banks and big business, defended the strongly attacked department stores and resisted anti-Semitic measures as bad for the economy.

In all three countries the emphasis on the exercise of strong power entailed centralization. Although the Soviet Union is nominally a federal republic, the Stalinist rule was centralist in character. The rights of the union republics were violated, nationalist sentiment equated with sedition and population transferred to other areas of the country. Constitutionally the Nazis centralized with the abolition of state parliaments, the subordination of the Länder to the Ministry of the Interior on January 30, 1934, the abolition of municipal diets on January 30, 1935, and the unification of the police for the whole of the Reich on June 16, 1936. In Italy the provincial executive committees were reformed, and the powers of prefects were extended in 1926. Within the party the Grand Council was nominated from the top, and it in turn chose the party secretary who appointed provincial secretaries.

Yet the process of centralization was less complete than these constitutional reforms suggest. Local loyalties in Germany remained strong, and the Gauleiters tended to reinforce these loyalties to expand their own power and defy central authority. In practice local administration had considerable autonomy from central authority. The Reichsstatthalters appointed in 1933 by Hitler to rule over local areas became independent of Berlin.[123] Not surprisingly, Goering refused to subordinate Prussia to the Reich Minister of the Interior. In Bavaria the state authorities saved the Church from the party.[124] Recent empirical studies show that in both Württemberg and Westphalia a certain degree of local self government and independence of action was preserved.[125]

Administration was itself haphazard. Even if his laziness and impatience were not major factors, Goering could not but neglect the multiplicity of offices he held. The Cabinet met infrequently and policy was often made without its knowledge. Hitler encouraged competition between ministers or appointed new agents to do work already assigned. The technical ministers like von Ruebenach might be nonparty members or like Fritz Todt, the builder of the autobahns, remarkably independent. The Minister of War was able to reach a compromise by which his officials would not engage actively in party work or party office.

PARTY AND STATE

Perhaps the most confusing element in at least two of the three systems is the relationship between party and state. The lack of clarity and of consistency in the relationship suggests even further qualification of the idea of the systems as monolithic entities.

The tactical compromises between Mussolini and the existing influential groups in Italy before he came to power meant that the monarchical, military, administrative, judicial, and clerical hierarchy retained their positions, for which the Fascist militants were not technically qualified. Continuity was maintained in the bureaucracy and judiciary. The traditional elite, some of whom later joined the party, coexisted with a Fascist leadership.[126] Parallel party institutions were created: the Grand Council alongside the Council of Ministers, the militia with the army, the party police with the regular police force, the federale (the provincial party secretaries) with the prefects.

Fascist leaders had spoken of the need for hierarchy, authority, and strong government, and expected these to be provided by their movement. But Mussolini soon decided that the party must not only be tamed but also be subordinated to the state. On June 13, 1923, he stated that "all party representatives are subordinate to the prefect": in the ninety-four provinces the federale were made subject to the prefect. The prefects were informed by Mussolini in 1927 that they, and not the party organs, were the official interpreters of the will of central government. The militia, which had the task of maintaining public order and premilitary training, had an ambiguous status in relation to the army. It increased in size, reaching about 750,000 by 1938. Its units fought in Spain and in Ethiopia in separate units from the army. Yet in spite of the tension that could be created by the militia, the army remained the strongest military force.

The party was to be an instrument of, rather than the leader of the state. The party did not itself take part in the determining of the purposes of government or the framing of policy though the secretary of the party had the rank of a cabinet minister. Party national and provincial leaders were appointed by the head of the government. Intransigent or extreme leaders were removed, and the power of local party secretaries curbed. The experiment in 1923 by which the alti commissari exercised both political and paramilitary authority was soon abandoned when Mussolini perceived it as a threat to his own position.[127] The Grand Council was created in 1922 as the supreme body of the party and became in December 1928 the constitutional organ "responsible for the coordination and integration of every activity of the regime," with a voice in the determination of the succession to the throne and the preparation of the list of deputies to be elected and union leaders to be appointed. In fact, however, it was accorded little power by Mussolini.

Although Hitler on March 22, 1933, said that "the work done outside the state organs was decisive," there was a confused picture on legislation, decision making, appointments, and jurisdictional boundaries between party and state. Although the party was able to veto governmental appointments and it was prominent at the district and local levels, it rarely initiated policies at the national level. About 60 percent of all governmental positions were held by party members, but two-thirds of these members had joined after 1933. The old fighters themselves, fanatical though they were in support of Hitler, lacked the necessary technical skills and administrative ability for state positions. Few in the party apparatus became governmental leaders, except the Gauleiters, who held dual positions at the local level. At the national level, apart from Hitler, the chief examples of dual leadership were Hess, Himmler, Rust, Ley, and Schirach.

Party as well as state was given legal power to act. The March 1933 Enabling Act, which handed over all legislative power to the government, was the basis for the legalizing of Nazi actions. The April 1935 law on local government, the January 1937 law on the civil service, the Nuremberg laws, and the occupancy and then abolition of the Presidency by Hitler in 1934, all supposedly gave legal approval to party intervention in state matters. The 1935 law made communal officials subject to supervision by the local party leaders as well as by the Reich Ministry of the Interior. The 1937 law made the appointments and promotions of civil servants subject to party approval. Civil servants who were party members were also subject to party courts. In spite of the law, however, the civil service was never completely a Nazi instrument; many senior civil servants never joined the party. Control over the life of officials was incomplete. Party organs shared public functions with governmental institutions. Education was partly controlled by the Hitler Youth, and public welfare was partly transferred to the NS-Public Welfare and the Winter Help which were allowed to collect money for charitable purposes. The Labor Front levied contributions based on the gross income of its members.

The December 1, 1933 law for the unity of party and state made the party the only political organization in Germany. The state accepted the party's definition of the racial issue: the office of Hess supervised the enforcement of the anti-Semitic legislation. Yet Hess's attempt as Deputy Führer to claim party superiority over the state and over decision making was only partly successful. In addition, the 1938 Nazi plan to control the personnel and budgets of the localities was a partial failure. By a 1937 law officials would report not to the party but to the Minister, who could then inform the party. On the whole, ministers successfully defended their administrative integrity.[128] The party could approve official appointments, and it influenced the administration of legislative and judicial matters, but it took little part in major pol-

itical decisions and never controlled national legislation. Practice did not bear out Hitler's
declaration at the 1934 party convention at
Nuremberg that "the state does not command us,
we command the state . . . we created the state."
The very complexity of the party structure, with
its large number of officials, with the Gauleiters
mostly opposing centralization, with its feuding
factions and bitter personal conflicts, both compli-
cated relations with the state and also helped prevent the direct subordination of the civil service.

Conflicting or overlapping jurisdictions were a
cause of confusion, as in the judicial field. In 1933
a special court, the Volksgerichtshof, was created
to try alleged treason cases, including listening to
foreign broadcasts. The Reich Minister of Justice
in November 1935 accepted the right of judicial
review by Hess,[129] who argued in 1938 that the
party could not be bound by legal norms in judg-
ing an individual. During the war the Minister
also allowed the party the right to deny permission for its leaders to testify in court proceedings.
A special judicial system was established in
October 1939 to deal with cases concerning the SS.
In police matters more harmony existed because
of the formal amalgamation in June 1936 of the
party post of Reichsführer-SS with the new office
of Chief of the German Police, with Himmler
occupying both positions.

This confusing and sometimes, as in the powers
of the HSSPF and the RSHA, bewildering pattern
of relations existed in the context of two other com-
plications. The first was the ultimate and final
power of Hitler, who in 1934 had transferred the
Presidential powers to himself as Führer. Under

the February 28, 1933 ordinance for an emergency situation, he could use the Gestapo as an instrument of his personal authority and permit protective custody, a political police force, and concentration camps. The claim of the party to represent the political will of the people was always secondary to the will of the Führer and his fulfillment of the German mission. The second complication was the rapid rise of the SS to a position of dominance which transcended both party and state. Its armed groups were not part of the police, the party, nor the Wehrmacht. The SS gradually superseded the state, making policy in foreign, military, and agricultural affairs and exemplifying the new elite, the biologically pure, obedient fighter. Among its other activities the SS extended its responsibilities to marriage authorizations, birth certificates, fire brigades, police courts and political education as well as to control over concentration camps. The SS became the executive agent of the will of the Führer to whom it was completely loyal, while the official machinery of the state concerned itself with routine business.[130] Its leader Himmler not only controlled all the local political police from 1934 and the national police from 1936, but was also Reich commissar for the strengthening of Germandom, the party representative for racial questions, and from 1943 the Minister of the Interior. The nature of his offices demonstrates that the SS was concerned with what was important to Hitler: the maintenance of his own power, anti-Semitism, lebensraum, the creation of a pure, strong Volk, and the elimination of opponents.

The problem of party-state relations in the
Soviet Union was different from in the other two
countries: it was the elimination of the party as a
policy making body. From Lenin's theory of party
organization, the concept of the dictatorship of the
proletariat became transmuted into that of the dictatorship of the Bolshevik party. Lenin in his
"Left-Wing" Communism—an Infantile Disorder
and Stalin in the *Foundations of Leninism*
claimed that no important political or organizational question was decided by any state institution without the guiding instructions of the
Central Committee of the party. In addition the
party was needed, according to Stalin in 1924, to
maintain the dictatorship of the proletariat, to
consolidate and expound it in order to achieve the
complete victory of socialism.[131] Unlike the Nazi
party, which was to be the master of public opinion, the Communist party would lead the masses,
disseminating and enforcing the goals of the
regime.[132] At the eighth party Congress in 1919
the Communist party was given a "leading role"
in the state, and the Politburo and Orgburo were
organized. From the collective secretariat established in 1920 Stalin emerged as General Secretary in 1922. At the tenth Congress in 1921 the
Central Control Commission was created with the
task of strengthening the unity and authority of
the party. Under Lenin the party leadership, a talented group who agreed on the need for party
unity, dominated the making of major policy decisions.[133] The party itself grew from 23,000 in January 1917 to 576,000 by January 1921. But the
highly personal dictatorship of Stalin meant rule

through cronies rather than through regular party channels.

The party was not reinstated to a prominent role until after Stalin. Between 1953 and 1958 Khrushchev managed to reassert the authority of the party in the face of possible challenge by the secret police, the army, and the state ministries. But after becoming prime minister in 1958, he too attempted to reduce the authority of the Central Committee, by inviting outside experts to its meetings. He increased the insecurity of party officials by his policy of a one-third turnover of the membership of party committees at elections, and caused confusion by the 1962 division of the regional committees into industrial and agricultural bodies. In addition, his reliance on a few advisers in a number of policy areas meant that both party and state were sometimes bypassed. But Khrushchev's general view was that "the party should play a strictly political role while technical questions should be left to the experts."[134]

Under Brezhnev the party has again been restored to a prominent position, asserting more control over the economy. In the new constitution passed in 1977, the party is defined as "the force that leads and directs Soviet society; it is the central element in the political system and in all the state and social organizations."

The party controls not only appointments in the party itself, but also, through the nomenklatura procedure, in industry, agriculture, education, and culture. Its responsibilities extend to all political, economic, and cultural activities in its area. The influence of local party organs on industry

depends on the interests of the first secretary of
the party, on the type of industry, and on the particular issue of decision making.[135]

The key variable in the relationship between
party and state is the territorial level. At the local
level the party is strong: it is concerned with long
range policy, though not with administrative
details. Nor can it force a higher state official to
act. The party function of checking the performance of the managers and providing guidance
has been enhanced in recent years by the better
technical training of party functionaries.

But the theory of the directing role of the party
conflicts with the industrial principle of one-man
management. Lower Soviet administrators themselves are not always clear about the proper relationship of the party organization to the plant
management.[136] In the complex Soviet administrative arrangement the essential image is that of
a policy making team within the enterprise.[137]

8

Ideology, Objectives, and Support

For the proponents of the totalitarian concept a troubling issue has always been the differences in the ideological convictions and purported objectives of the three systems. If the differences are regarded as meaningful and the ideology taken seriously, it would be difficult to regard the three systems as members of a common class. Arendt argued that beyond the senselessness of totalitarian society is "enthroned the ridiculous supersense of its ideological superstition."[138]

Both the Soviet Union and Nazi Germany, if not Fascist Italy, claimed an understanding of the nature and requirements of world history and suggested that their regimes would be based on that understanding: for the Soviet Union, the will of the proletariat and of liberated people, for the

Nazis the will of the stronger and the destiny of the German people. Historical necessity would prevail over both legal standards and ethical norms.[139]

There is no problem about the ideology of the Soviet Union. Supposedly based on Marxism-Leninism, the Stalinist era has been explained or defended by the need to create those conditions necessary for the building of a socialist society. The only difficulty, therefore, is to ascertain whether the Stalinist practice was in any way related to that need, or based on ideological conviction. The psychology or motivation of Stalin thus becomes the crucial issue.

It is more difficult to come to grips with the other two regimes and to assess their position on the left-right spectrum of politics. Both had come to power in particular historical circumstances: an economic and psychological crisis produced by the war, increased anxiety of the lower middle class, fear of social revolution, heightened nationalist sentiments, a large number of veterans who could not adjust to peace and craved violent actions, the prevalence of such illegal violence.[140] Both were essentially negative in character in their rejection of liberalism, individualism, equality, humanistic values, and internationalism. Salvatorelli called Fascism the anti-risorgimento and Malaparte referred to it as counter-reformation. Both systems were consciously elitist in their stress on the few destined to rule, authoritarian in their insistence that power is hierarchically exercised from the top down, and monist in their emphasis on a unity and discipline binding their population and embracing all interests. Both emphasized strength and despised weakness. Both thought a strong military presence essential not simply to preserve traditional values but as an aggressive, militant force. Both had an economic system in which the market was preserved but which was characterized by control over major economic policy and the subordination of the entrepreneurial class to public or party officials. Both attempted to mobilize the masses who had previously been neglected as a political force and who could be deluded to believe they had a direct relationship with the leader. Both appealed to a basic myth, the will of the individual leader, race, or nation. Both stressed action and violence, not simply as a way of solving problems but also, in Sorelian fashion, as an elevating and creative experience. Inactivity, said Mussolini, is death. Hitler continually talked of sacrifice and of struggle "as the father of all things," the iron law of German historical development. For Mussolini war alone could bring human energies up to their highest tension and put "the stamp of nobility on the peoples who have the courage to meet it." For Hitler pacificism paralyzed "the natural strength of the self-preservation of people." Only through fighting have individual states and the world as a whole become great. Life was a cruel struggle and had no other object but the preservation of the species. The life of the individual, he said, must not be set at too high a price.[141] Economic programs were referred to in military terms: "the battle of wheat," "the battle of the lira." Both regimes appealed to nonrational or antirational elements with their emphasis on parades, demonstrations, symbols, uniforms, strong colors, youth, and "thinking with the blood."

Few have held that Fascism had any serious philosophic basis, though Mack Smith's view that the technique of using castor oil was its only original contribution is extreme.[142] Mussolini himself acknowledged that faith was more decisive than the doctrine noticeably absent in Fascism. Mussolini came to power as head of a protean movement including populists, workers, industrialists, students, monarchists, and republicans, without any precise program or ideology, and was proud of his ability to improvise. He soon gave up his revolutionary socialism and reached compromises with the traditional elites. Perhaps he was genuinely interested in increasing production. Much more central for him was a strong state, nationalism, since the highest reality was the nation organized in the state, and imperial conquest.

Mussolini spoke of "the single, unitary state," which was not only "the sole repository of all the history" of Italy, but also a moral idea. In his famous article in the Italian Encyclopedia in 1932, he wrote that "everything is in the state, and nothing human or spiritual exists . . . outside the state. In this sense fascism is totalitarian." Mussolini spoke of men's "imminent relationship with a superior and objective will that transcends the particular individual," and of the coincidence of the individual with the state which is "the conscience and universal will of man in his historical existence." Gentile, Mussolini's philosophical ghost writer, saw Fascism as embracing all human activity: "it is impossible to be Fascist in politics, and non-Fascist . . . in school, non-Fascist in our families, non-Fascist in our daily occupations."[143] For Gentile the maximum of liberty coincided with the maximum of state force. From a practical point of view, the state was the means by which discipline could be imposed over both the squadristi and the party, thereby reinforcing the personal power of Mussolini. But a strong state was also the vehicle by which Italy, which many Fascists felt had been betrayed by her allies at the Versailles peace conference, could deservedly expand in the Balkans or in Africa.

The two terms in national socialism were not of equivalent value. The socialist components in the original twenty-five point Nazi program— abolition of unearned income, nationalization of all joint stock corporations or trusts, introduction of profit sharing in big business, nationalization of big department stores, "the destruction of interest-slavery"—remained unfulfilled. In a tactical move to gain rural electoral support Article 17 of the program had been amended in 1928 to remove the threat of the expropriation of peasant property. The revolutionary impulse in Nazism had virtually ended with Feder and the Strassers. In its place was an amalgam of ideas and themes—racism, social Darwinism, nationalism, expansionism—and a mixture of fears, hatreds, and prejudices, of which the chief were anti-Semitism, xenophobia, anti-Communism, and an antibourgeois attitude. Rauschning's argument[144] that national socialism was a nihilistic movement which supposed revolutionaries used for personal power is only partly true. At its core was the idea of the fulfillment of the destiny of the German people, which meant a pure Volk, the conquest of Eastern Europe, and above all the elimination of Jews.

A crucial difference between the Fascist and Nazi system was the emphasis of the latter on the Volk rather than on the state. The German people, wherever they were physically, were to be viewed as an organic unit tied together in blood relationships and linked by a natural harmony of interests. The mystical, vague concept of the Volk would help create an integral nationalism binding diverse groups together and support the elimination of hostile forces and institutions. For Hitler the state was not, as it was for Mussolini, "a moral concept or the realization of an absolute idea," but was "the servant of the racial people." The state had to regard the preservation and intensification of the race as its highest task. Opposing the "Jewish Christ creed with its effeminate pity ethics" Hitler wrote of his "strong, heroic belief in God in Nature, God in our own people, in our destiny in our blood." In Hitler's anti-Semitic diatribes Jews were attacked as parasites, as maggots in a rotting body, as people whose bloodstreams carried poison into every limb and polluted the Volk.[145]

The insistent Nazi claim to lebensraum combined theoretical propositions and practical function. Some of the fundamental ideas of Nazism—life as struggle, racial theory, the hierarchy of peoples—gave lebensraum a pseudo-philosophical basis. The higher German Kultur would replace the inferior Slavic one. But it was also useful in creating a national consensus in pursuit of territorial acquisition, especially in Eastern Europe. In addition it would both ensure sufficient food and oil supplies for Germany itself and be the basis for German colonization of inferior peoples. Hitler's grand design in foreign policy would start with war against France, but the ultimate war would be against Russia.[146] The great German empire would be reestablished by conquering Eastern Europe, to which Germany was entitled. This territorial acquisition would also satisfy Hitler's dreams of vast spaces. Life, he explained, enabled him "to give the dream reality . . . Space lends wings to (the) imagination."

There was a specious rationale to Nazi anti-Semitism. Jews could be attacked as despoilers through intermarriage of German blood, who must be purged to purify the Volk. Their removal would ensure the unity of the nation. Jewishness could be equated with materialism and Jews regarded as controllers of international finance. They could be seen either as the supporters of democracy, liberalism, and selfish individualism, or as the standardbearers of decadent modern culture. They could be opposed as the leading figures or originators of the socialist movement or as architects of the Bolshevik revolution, which was itself part of a larger Jewish conspiracy. They could be attacked because this was the easiest way to arouse the enthusiasm and irrationalism of the population.

Yet all these arguments cannot account for the intensity of the animosity or the extremism of the anti-Semitic activity ending with the Holocaust.

Anti-Semitism was probably the only belief to which Hitler subscribed unreservedly and which preoccupied him personally and politically. One ingenious explanation is that it stemmed from his belief that his mother had been poisoned in the course of treatment for cancer by a Jewish doctor in 1907, a belief that was reinforced after he was gassed during World War I in 1918.[147] By his own testimony it was in 1908 that he changed from "a feeble cosmopolite . . . into a fanatical anti-Semite." At the beginning of his political career, in a letter of September 16, 1919, Hitler wrote that the "ultimate goal must unalterably be the elimination of the Jews altogether." He was always talking of a "thorough" solution or of "the removal of the Jews from the midst of our people." He complained that the thousands of Jews he held responsible for the defeat of Germany in World War I had not been gassed. In *Mein Kampf* he wrote, "In standing guard against the Jew I am defending the handiwork of the Lord."[148] Freeing Germany of Jews would be liberating the world from a great danger. He ended his life with the same conviction. In 1943 he told Admiral Horthy that "Jews must be treated like tuberculosis bacilli" and that such "a bestial species" should not be preserved.[149] In his last conversation on April 2, 1945, he said the world "will be eternally grateful that I have extinguished the Jews in Germany." His final words in the testament of April 29, 1945 were his "implacable opposition against the universal poisoner of all peoples, international Jewry."

The anti-Jewish persecution began immediately after his acquisition of power in 1933 with the boycott of Jewish shops, goods, doctors, and lawyers, and the exclusion of Jews from civil service and other professions. The civil rights of Jews were abolished. The 1935 Nuremberg laws declared that no Jew could be a citizen of the Reich, nor marry anyone with Aryan blood. By 1938 identity cards were required of Jews. The November 9, 1938 Kristallnacht, the centrally directed and nation-wide wave of anti-Semitism, resulted not only in the destruction of synagogues and Jewish shops, but also led to the imposition of a fine on the Jewish communities. In September 1939 the final goal seemed to be the transfer of Jews to the East. At some point after this Hitler decided on the physical destruction of Jews. Economic needs were to be ignored if attending to them prevented dealing with the Jewish problem. Resources which might have been used to send troops to fight on the eastern front were used to send Jews to the extermination camps. On July 31, 1941 Heydrich was given the task of arranging for "the total solution" of the Jewish question. On February 24, 1943 Hitler said that the struggle would end with the extirpation of Judaism in Europe. The result was the murder of 6 million Jew by the gas chambers or executions in the concentration camps or by the SS Einsatz-gruppen in Eastern Europe.

Hitler directly influenced Mussolini in this anti-Semitic policy. Most analysts agree that racism was an insignificant feature of Italian Fascist theory until the mid 1930s. Mussolini in 1935 became concerned about racial matters with the cohabitation between Italian soldiers and natives in Ethiopia. Though Fascist concern was always about the nation, not the race, some racial theories were developed to justify the imperial policy of expansion in Africa. The Manifesto of Italian racism issued in 1938 stated that the Italian race was ready to fulfill its historic purpose. But racial policy took a new departure with the increasing attacks by Jews throughout the world against the Italian invasion of Ethiopia. Mussolini adopted a more anti-Semitic position, especially when he found himself supported by certain elements in the church.[150] But whereas anti-Semitism was the crucial element for Hitler, it was still relatively unimportant for Mussolini until the entente between them. Some of Mussolini's best friends were Jewish women, and he even occasionally supported Zionism, though in the militant Revisionist version of Jabotinsky. Under Hitler's influence, a decree of November 1938 prohibited mixed marriages and barred Jews from all sectors of public life, though some categories such as veterans were exempt.

The constituencies to which the German and Italian movements originally appealed and the interests the regimes sought to satisfy were at once similar because of their common antiliberalism and different because of the different elements in their ideologies and programs, the rigidity with which those ideologies were held, and the different manner in which power had been captured.

Nazism has commonly been assumed to have been a movement of the lower middle class or a rejection of modernity. Certainly it appealed to that class with its programs of protection, autarky, higher tariffs for agriculture, elimination of Jewish department stores, assertion of law and order, and preservation of the social order. The strongest correlation in Nazi electoral support at the last elections under Weimar was with Protestants in small towns and with the self-employed in handicrafts; the weakest was with blue collar workers.[151] In 1930 the largest single occupational group among the Nazis in the Reichstag were white collar workers. In the last years of Weimar this social class, like the self-employed and the farmers, was disproportionately over represented among Nazi party members and voters.[152] Yet to call Nazism a petty-bourgeois phenomenon may be misleading. Merkl, in his study of the 581 cases of the Abel survey, has argued that the usual class, economic, and ideological explanations may be too simplistic.[153] The chief support came not only from those who disliked modern industrial society and feared big business and big labor but also towards the end of the 1920s from those who felt humiliated by German defeat in 1918 and from the military desperadoes, in Sauer's term.[154] At a regional election of 1929 the Nazi gains came from the German National Party.[155] The quintessence of Nazism was violence and aggression.

Similarly, Fascism attracted not only the urban and rural lower middle class including state employees, and those who feared that democracy and parliamentarism were irrelevant and incapable of ensuring social order and discipline, but also the exservicemen who had experienced a comradeship of the trenches in the War. This moral aristocracy wanted to recreate the lost community in peacetime; temperamentally it yearned for excit-

ing action in the squadristi. Though it attracted
exsocialists and revolutionary syndicalists who
favored an anticapitalist society, and though de
Felice takes Mussolini's early socialism seriously
and argues both that Fascism transformed the old
political structure by bringing in a new class to
power and that Mussolini believed in a progressive future, Fascism can only paradoxically be
called a movement of the political left. Like
Nazism, Fascism came to power in a society where
preindustrial elites such as the landed aristocracy,
military leadership, bureaucracy, and the church
had preserved their position in an industrial era,
but in Italy these elites were more influential than
in Germany. Fascism was a more complex phenomenon than Nazism, with its heterogenity of
goals and appeal to both reactionary and revolutionary sentiments, to agricultural and urban
interests, and to northern and southern parts of
the country, partly because of the vagueness of its
intentions and partly because of Mussolini's tactical ability.[156] De Felice has suggested that, whereas Nazism was always right-wing in character,
Fascism could be regarded as stemming from the
Enlightenment tradition. But both Nazism and
Fascism eliminated their radical elements in their
desire to stabilize the economic and social order.

IDEOLOGY AND PRACTICE

There was considerable discrepancy between
ideology and actual policy in the systems. In Germany the promised society of small traders, small
farmers, and small towns faded before industrial

concentration. In Berlin alone about 10,000 shops and stores had disappeared by 1939. The Nazis never destroyed non-Jewish department stores; they did not abolish consumers' cooperatives until 1941. Hitler may have been opposed to an industrial society, but he laid the groundwork for the transition of the German social structure to modernity by reducing traditional loyalties.[157] Early Nazi propaganda had stressed the merit of peasants—whom Hitler once called "the cornerstone of the whole nation"—the superiority of rural life and values, the significance of folklore, the prevention of migration to the "soulless" cities, the concept of Blüt und Boden. (In similar fashion the Fascist regime in 1931 and 1939 passed laws forbidding rural workers to move to towns of over 25,000 or to provincial capitals important for industry.) But German society became more highly urbanized. The dream of the colonization of Eastern Europe and of the creation of a new nobility based on purity of blood and race gave way before the need for Eastern European labor. Women's place was to be in the home. The battlefield for women was different from that of men. With each child brought into the nation the woman "is fighting on behalf of the nation." But though women were excluded from all leading positions in the Nazi hierarchy and married women doctors and civil servants dismissed at an early stage, the pace of women's employment was quickened and their status improved with the demand for labor. Ironically, history contradicted Hitler's aims, with the creation of a Jewish state in Israel, the advance of the Soviet Union into East-

ern Europe, the independence of colonial countries, and a social democratic regime in Germany.

In similar fashion the proclaimed Soviet
ideals—egalitarianism, the withering away of the
state, abolition of the family, end of alienation and
specialization, the social power of the
proletariat—have vanished before the Stalinist
reality of wage differentials, repression by a
stronger state, the continuation of family ties,
technological specialization, and the dictatorial
power of the proletariat.

A COMMON GENUS

Notwithstanding the different doctrinal bases
of the three systems, in practice there was, in
Trotsky's phrase, "a deadly similarity" among
them.[158] With the partial exception of Italy from
these generalizations, they were similar in their
total elimination of political freedom, in the power-
lessness of their voluntary organizations, in the
unregulated power of their secret police, in their
pretense to understand history and execute its
laws, in their assumption that human nature was
malleable by the regime, in their endless process of
indoctrination, in their emphasis on hierarchical
leadership, in their demand for unquestioning
obedience, in their stress on sacrifice for the good
of the whole or on behalf of the future, in their pretense of mass approval, in their drive to mobilize
the populations, in the dominant position of their
individual dictators, in their portrayal of
"enemies"—Jews in Germany, Marxists in Italy,
destroyers in Russia—who must be purged, in

their relentless use of terror, in their effort to attain autarky, in their destruction of free labor organizations, in their secular ideology or beliefs, in their use of planning, in their one party system or movement, in their belief in a strong exercise of political power. Their fundamental antiliberalism and their acceptance of coercion and violence as a norm rather than an exception distinguishes them from democratic systems, no matter how much they purport to be concerned with the liberation of the whole people or of humanity.

From an empirical perspective, the regimes were also similar in party organization and in propaganda techniques, taking account of their different economic and cultural levels. The Leninist party and the Nazi movement were both based on a democratic centralism that was dictatorial. The Nazi block leader paralleled the Soviet agitator at the local level. Both systems used elections or plebiscites to dramatize approval of imposed policy. Both controlled leisure activities through official organs. Both penetrated the private lives of citizens by use of welfare services as well as by processes of socialization.

9

From Totalitarianism To Authoritarianism

A remaining problem is that of assessing whether the Soviet Union in the post-Stalin years can still be accurately described as totalitarian. Most commentators on that country in recent years have not thought it a useful term, though others are prepared to use a modified phrase such as "rationalized" or "populist" or "mature" totalitarianism.[159] The view that the regime has changed to a kind of authoritarianism is based on the diminution of arbitrary terror as a means of obtaining compliance, the ability of nonparty groups to make their voice heard in decision making, and the logical prerequisites of an industrial society that has experienced the growth of a managerial group and of consumer interests as well as educational advancement and scientific accomplishment.

Clearly, terror of the Stalinist variety has declined, and party control has been rationalized. More emphasis is placed on material incentives and on individual rewards and less on the demand for sacrifice and on the making of revolution from above. But the Soviet Union has followed an uneven rather than a constant course, with limited forms of coercion replacing unrestricted terror and with predictable rather than arbitrary control as under Stalin. Though tolerance has varied from year to year, the expression of dissent has been permitted up to a point, provided it does not extend to outright opposition. A legal facade has been given to the prosecution of political dissenters, some of whom have been allowed to emigrate or been exiled. A present and future leadership that has not been involved in the revolutionary struggles, and most of whom have matured since the Stalinist terror, is likely to be less ruthless than Stalin and more likely to be restrained by "socialist legality." Pragmatic administration of the existing system is more the norm than ideological implementation of a future utopia.

Terror of the Stalinist kind has not affected the ruling group itself. Though it has oscillated between personal and collective rule—Khrushchev indicated that under him there was at least consultation if not collective decision making[160]—the leadership has imposed some self constraints. Since Beria, all agree that no violence will be used against a member of the leadership and that no one will publicly advance himself as a spokesman for a particular interest or position. The first secretary of the party should not also be prime minister, though secretary Brezhnev did become President of the state in 1977. There has been a remarkable stability of the Soviet leadership in the Politburo, the Central Committee, and in the Council of Ministers under Brezhnez when compared with the dramatic changes after the deaths of Lenin and Stalin. No great purges in the party have occurred though the ousters of Khrushchev in 1964 and Podgorny, the Chairman of the Supreme Soviet, in 1977 were never officially explained. Some decentralization and policy making has been allowed to the regional parties, which can define problems and formulate solutions pertinent to local conditions.[161]

But the party is still based on the principles of democratic centralism and on the acceptance of the unconditionally binding nature of the decisions of the higher organs on lower ones. Party secretaries in reality are still named from above in spite of the formal election procedure. The first secretaries of some of the regional party organs, at least through the years of Khrushchev's power, remain selected and removed by the central authorities. The current party leader Brezhnev, perhaps to prevent the emergence of an alternative power group, brought the leaders of the police and the armed forces into the party leadership.

Because of the doctrine of the dictatorship of the proletariat that prevents alternative leadership, and the principle of democratic centralism that restricts important decision making to a small elite, the Soviet Union, as a model of totalitarianism, appeared to be devoid of internal pressures, let alone dissent. Dallin has commented that this denial of actual or latent diversity and variety is the single most characteristic bias in analyses of the Soviet Union.[162] Recent analysts, of whom Skilling has been the most penetrating, have argued that different categories of political groups of like-minded individuals—leadership or factional, official, intellectual, social and opinion groups—have had some ability and opportunity to articulate interests, though they have lacked formal organization.[163] In this view Soviet "consultative authoritarianism" entails attending to the voices of these groups. They can influence policy-making in the party and state administration because of their specialized knowledge, which is available through the increasing recruitment of technical specialists in the upper levels of the party and in the standing committees of the Supreme Soviet, through the consultation of expert groups by the party secretariat, and by the opening of the process to discussion of certain issues for limited periods.[164] Decisions may thus be made on the basis of technical advice and orderly administration, and bargaining can take place within the highly centralized system.[165] Even within the system the regional parties have some autonomy and discretion in handling local problems. This does not approximate pluralism in the Western sense of autonomy of groups or of competing allegiances that may lead to political opposition.[166] Yet the recognition that groups other than the proletariat existed led Khrushchev to redefine the Soviet Union as "a state of all the people" and the Communist party in similar fashion. The national anthem, revised in 1977, stresses the role of the party as the leader and inspiration of all the people.

The logic of industrial organization suggests the relaxation of some controls to ensure greater efficiency. The indispensability of scientific research entails a certain amount of intellectual freedom. The need to satisfy the wants of a society with an increasing standard of living and the necessity for greater foreign trade suggest that economic performance will be the test of administrative work. In general the more talented individuals seem more likely to enter into a technical or administrative career than a political one.[167] Fischer argues that senior political positions will in future be filled by those with technical training.[168] A trend of this kind has already been shown by the developmental rationality and technical capabilities present at the regional level.[169]

Yet it is not automatic that the increasing importance of scientists and engineers or the significance of a professional and managerial group will lead to major changes in the nature of the system, or that these specialists and administrators, subjected still to political indoctrination, will constitute a critical voice calling for greater political freedom or for controls on the exercise of state power. Advocates of the convergence thesis have been premature in suggesting that the industrial and technological advances in the United States and the Soviet Union may lead to similar social systems in the two countries. The view that a modernized and technologically sophisticated society requires a constitutional political system would seem to be an improbable version of economic determinism.

There is always cause for hesitation in analyz-
ing the Soviet Union. Stalin's body may have been
removed from the Lenin-Stalin mausoleum in Red
Square in 1961 but his spirit has not entirely evap-
orated. Mass terror may have ended, but strong
controls, concentration of political power dictatorship remain with the use of intimidation, mental
hospitals for political purposes, exile of dissenters,
threat of dismissal from work, expulsion from
unions, arbitrary punishment to some degree,
social ostracism, involuntary interruption of
careers, transfer of people to remote areas of the
country, residential controls, and concentration
camps. Elections for all Soviet institutions and to
all leading party bodies are a formality, and elitist
methods prevail in the running of the party and
country.[170] The Supreme Soviet and its Presidium
exist for little more than display. It has never
introduced a legislative bill on its own initiative
nor rejected one sent to it by the real rulers. The
system is still a highly centralized one dominated
by one nationality in a multinational land in
which the individual republics lack any meaningful right of self determination. There has been no
general granting of freedom. If more freedom has
been permitted in the fields of genetics, biology,
agronomy, and economics since the fall of
Khrushchev, less has been permitted in the area of
creative literature. Public expression of dissent
has been punished by imprisonment in labor
camps and asylums. Nonconformity has been cas-
tigated as a form of mental disease or a sign of
"paranoid tendencies."[171] Well known psychia-
trists have collaborated with the secret police to
commit political or religious dissidents to mental

hospitals,[172] where about ten percent of the inmates are said to be political cases.

The secret police, in the form of the KGB still exists, with 90,000 officers and over 300,000 employees. The head of the KGB, Yuri Andropov, is a member of the Politburo, and the representation of the KGB in the bureaus of the parties in the Soviet republics has increased. There are still about 900 labor camps containing over a million prisoners. The Gulag of Solzhenitsyn has been replaced by Gumz, a subdivision of the Ministry of Internal Affairs. The death penalty has been restored for economic crimes. There have been waves of anti-Semitism in 1962-63 and 1970-71, and show trials in 1973.

Controls are still regarded as essential: as Khrushchev explained in 1962, "control is above all order." It was noticeable in Khrushchev's 1956 speech that he condemned Stalin's destruction of the Communist party but not his slaughter of millions of nonparty members. The party remains in monopoly control of information and communication, and regulates all organizations. An article of the new constitution adopted in 1977 states that agitation or propaganda to undermine or weaken Soviet power, and the distribution of slanderous fabrications against the Soviet state and social system, are crimes punishable by up to seven years in prison. Economic planning is still maintained. The proposals of Liberman for economic change by using profit as a yardstick for performance were neglected after 1969.

A complex relationship now exists among the communist countries. At the 1956 party congress Khrushchev argued that each socialist country would follow its own road to socialism. But they were to remain loyal to Marxism-Leninism and to proletarian internationalism. The post-Stalin leaders have used force when necessary to keep the East European countries in line. But they have also used other methods such as the appointment of senior party and state personnel, especially those trained in the Soviet Union, and the integration of the other countries in both economic arrangements such as COMECON and military organizations such as the command structure of the Warsaw Pact.

The bureaucratization of the revolutionary elite may have occurred, but it is inadequate to regard the Soviet Union merely as a conservative, bureaucratic system. To view the regime as a giant corporation is to imply that problems are dealt with in a rational manner from which coercion is absent, and is to ignore the way in which both ends and means are chosen. T. H. Rigby has indicated[173] some of the major problems with this view. It does not sufficiently appreciate the complex relationship and overlapping jurisdiction of party and governmental organs. Decisions between competing choices are made more in response to the current priorities and preoccupations of the most important relevant organization than on the basis of formal rationality. And, in order to achieve some desired objective, mobilization may mean redeployment of people from their normal tasks to the detriment of rational administration. Rigby himself has usefully analyzed the Soviet Union as a "mono-organizational" society in which most activities are directed by hierar-

chies of appointed officials under the direction of a
single command, and which has a monopolistic
and comprehensive ideology, coercive social controls and a crypto-politics in which bureaucrats
engage. Individual dictatorship, in this view, may
have been useful for the establishment of a mono-
organizational society but is not logically required
for its perpetuation. The dilemma still remains of
how controls can be limited in a system in which a
monopoly of power exists.

The case of the contemporary Soviet Union is
useful for concluding this discussion. Totalitarianism has been a valuable term for designating
the uniqueness of limited number of systems at a
specific moment in modern history. Their style,
organizational devices, and political structures
differentiate the three countries from authoritarian regimes such as Franco Spain or Portugal
under Salazar. The relationship between the rulers and the ruled separates them from military
regimes or despotic dictatorships or outright
tyrannies such as that of Idi Amin in Uganda.
Their Western nature, historical continuity, economic position, and technological controls distin-
guish them from the one party systems of the Afro-
Asian countries. Perhaps one might talk of a
regime being "more" or "less" totalitarian in
nature,[174] but this would not be particularly help-
ful for classificatory purposes. The experience of
the Soviet Union suggests the conclusion that a
totalitarian system so highly dependent on particular individuals, can transform itself into something sufficiently less severe, that it can be
characterized in a different way.

Notes

1. Herbert H. Rowen, "L'Etat c'est moi: Louis XIV and the State," *French Historical Studies* 2 no. 1 (1961): 92.
2. George Simmel, *The Sociology of George Simmel,* translated by Kurt H. Wolff (New York: Free Press, 1950), pp. 90-91, 203.
3. Hannah Arendt, "The Origins of Totalitarianism," *Review of Politics* 15 (1953): 81.
4. Hans Buchheim, *Totalitarian Rule: Its Nature and Characteristics* (Middletown: Wesleyan University Press, 1968), p. 69.
5. Karl Popper, *The Open Society and Its Enemies* (Princeton: Princeton University Press, 1966).
6. Jacob Talmon, *The Origins of Totalitarian Democracy* (London: Secker, 1952).
7. Herbert Marcuse, *One Dimensional Man* (Boston: Beacon Press, 1964).
8. L.K. Adler and T.G. Paterson, "Red Fascism: The Merger of Nazi Germany and Soviet Russia in the American Image of Totalitarianism, 1930s-1950s," *American Historical Review* 75 (1970): 1046-64.
9. Francesco Nitti, *Bolshevism, Fascism, and Democracy* (New York: Macmillan, 1927), pp. 70-127.
10. Alexander Kaczmarek, "Religion and Totalitarianism," *Contemporary Review* 222 (1973): 282.
11. Alexsandr Solzhenitsyn, *The Gulag Archipelago* (New York: Harper & Row, 1974).
12. Roy A. Medvedev, *Let History Judge* (New York: Knopf, 1971); and "New Pages from a Political Biography of

Stalin" in *Stalinism: Essays in Historical Interpretation,* ed. Robert C. Tucker (New York: Norton, 1977), p. 205.

13. M.M. Drachkovitch, *De Karl Marx à Léon Blum* (Geneva: Droz, 1954), p. 66.

14. Robert C. Tucker, "Stalinism as Revolution from Above," in Tucker, pp. 81-82.

15. Roy A. Medvedev, *On Socialist Democracy* (New York: Norton, 1977), p. 174.

16. Ibid., p. 127.

17. T.H. Rigby, "Stalinism and the Mono-Organizational Society," in Tucker, pp. 67-68.

18. Ernest Clark, "Revolutionary Ritual: A Comparative Analysis of Thought Reform and the Show Trial," *Studies in Comparative Communism* 9 (1976): 236, 242.

19. Richard Pipes, *Russia under the Old Regime* (London: Weidenfeld & Nicolson, 1974); Tucker, pp. 99-100; Moshe Lewin, "The Social Background of Stalinism," in Tucker, p. 127.

20. Roy A. Medvedev and Zhores A. Medvedev, *Khrushchev: The Years in Power* (New York: Norton, 1978), p. 38.

21. Nikolai Tolstoy, *Victims of Yalta* (London: Hodder & Stoughton, 1978).

22. Robert Conquest, *The Great Terror: Stalin's Purge of the Thirties* (New York: Macmillan, 1968), pp. 532-33.

23. Maurice Merleau-Ponty, *Humanisme et terreur* (Paris: Gallimard, 1947).

24. Kendall E. Bailes, "The Politics of Technology: Stalin and Technocratic Thinking among Soviet Engineers," *American Historical Review* 79 (1974): 445-69.

25. Aryeh Unger, "Stalin's Renewal of the Leading Stratum: A note on the Great Purge," *Soviet Studies* 20 (1969): 321-30.

26. E.H. Carr, *Socialism in One Country, 1924-1926,* vol. 1 (London: Macmillan, 1958), p. 185; Isaac Deutscher, *Stalin: A Political Biography* (New York: Oxford University Press, 1949), pp. 318-22.

27. George Kennan, *Memoirs* (Boston: Little, Brown, 1967), pp. 503-4.

28. Robert C. Tucker, "The Dictator and Totalitarianism,"
     World Politics 17 (1965): 555-83.
29. Stephen F. Cohen, "Bolshevism and Stalinism," in
     Tucker, *Stalinism,* pp. 24-25.
30. James Millar and Alec Nove, "Was Stalin Really Neces-
     sary?" *Problems of Communism* 25 no. 4 (1976): 49-62.
31. Moshe Lewin, " 'Taking Grain': Soviet Policies of Agri-
     cultural Procurements before the War," in *Essays in
     Honour of E.H. Carr,* ed. C. Abramsky (Hamden:
     Archon, 1974), p. 316.
32. Stephen F. Cohen, "Bolshevism and Stalinism: New
     Reflections on an old Problem," *Dissent* 24 (1977): 190-
     205.
33. Tucker, *Stalinism,* pp. 96-97.
34. Bertrand Russell, *Bolshevism: Practice and Theory*
     (New York: Harcourt, 1920); Franz Borkenau, "Zur Sozi-
     ologie des Faschismus," *Archiv fur Sozialwissen-
     schaften and Sozialpolitik* 1 (1933): 513-47.
35. Robert C. Tucker, "Towards a Comparative Politics of
     Movement-Regimes," *American Political Science
     Review* 55 (1961): 281-89.
36. Robert C. Tucker, "Paths of Communist Revolution,
     1917-1967," in *The Soviet Union: A Half Century of
     Communism,* ed. Kurt London (Baltimore: Johns Hop-
     kins Press, 1968), p. 9.
37. David Apter, *The Politics of Modernization* (Chicago:
     University of Chicago Press, 1965), pp. 360-61.
38. Joseph Stalin, *Foundations of Leninism* (New York:
     International Publishers, 1932).
39. Joseph Stalin, *Leninism,* 2 vols. (London: Allen &
     Unwin, 1928, 1933).
40. Naum Jasny, *Soviet Industrialization, 1928-1952* (Chi-
     cago: University of Chicago Press, 1961), pp. 77, 90, 99,
     105-6.
41. Tucker, *Stalinism,* p. 98.
42. Michael P. Gehlen, *The Communist Party of the Soviet
     Union: A Functional Analysis* (Bloomfield: Indiana
     University Press, 1969), p. 75.
43. Richard Lowenthal, "Development v. Utopia in Com-
     munist Policy," in *Change in Communist Systems,* ed.
     Chalmers Johnson (Stanford: Stanford University

Press, 1970), pp. 33-116.

44. A. James Gregor, *The Fascist Persuasion in Radical Politics* (Princeton: Princeton University Press, 1974), p. 178.

45. A James Gregor, "Fascism and Modernization," *World Politics* 26 (1974): 378.

46. Adrian Lyttleton, *The Seizure of Power: Fascism in Italy, 1919-1929* (London: Weidenfeld & Nicolson, 1973), p. 433.

47. Arnold Hughes and Martin Kolinsky, "Paradigmatic Fascism and Modernization: A Critique," *Political Studies* 24 (1976): 371-96; George Hildebrand, *Growth and Structure in the Economy of Modern Italy* (Cambridge, Mass.: Harvard University Press, 1965).

48. Roland Sarti, "Fascist Modernization in Italy: Traditional or Revolutionary?," *American Historical Review* 75 (1970): 1029-45.

49. Edward R. Tannenbaum, *Fascism in Italy* (New York: Basic Books, 1972), p. 74.

50. Joseph Goebbels, *The Goebbels Diaries, 1942-1943* (Garden City: Doubleday, 1948), p. 468.

51. Denis Mack Smith, *Mussolini's Roman Empire* (London: Longman, 1976).

52. Renzo de Felice, *Fascism: An Informal Introduction to Its Theory and Practice* (New Brunswick: Transaction, 1977), p. 31.

53. Luigi Barzini, *The Italians* (New York: Atheneum, 1965), p. 137.

54. Giovanni Gentile, "L'unità di Mussolini," *Corriére della Sera,* 15 May 1934, quoted in H.S. Harris, *The Social Philosophy of Giovanni Gentile* (Urbana: University of Illinois Press, 1960), p. 219.

55. Dietrich Orlow, *The History of the Nazi Party, 1919-1933* (Pittsburgh: University of Pittsburgh Press, 1969), pp. 75-80.

56. Donald M. McKale, *The Nazi Party Courts: Hitler's Management of Conflict in His Movement, 1921-1945* (Lawrence: University of Kansas Press, 1974).

57. Albert Speer, *Spandau: The Secret Diaries* (New York: Macmillan, 1976), pp. 49, 81-82, 139.

58. Dietrich Orlow, *The History of the Nazi Party, 1933-1945* (Pittsburgh: University of Pittsburgh Press, 1973), p. 7.
59. Joseph Nyomarkay, *Charisma and Factionalism in the Nazi Party* (Minneapolis: University of Minneapolis Press, 1967), p. 5.
60. Brian Horrocks et al., *Corps Commander* (London: Sidgwick & Jackson, 1977).
61. Karl D. Bracher, *The German Dictatorship* (New York: Praeger, 1972), pp. 341-42.
62. Alan Bullock, *Hitler: A study in Tyranny* (New York: Harper & Row, 1962).
63. Joachim C. Fest, "Thinking about Hitler," *Encounter* 45 (1975): 81-91; Fest, *Hitler* (New York: Harcourt, Brace, Jovanovich, 1973).
64. Robert G.L. Waite, *The Psychopathic God: Adolf Hitler* (New York: Basic Books, 1977), pp. xvi, 356-58, 372.
65. Antonio Gramsci, *The Modern Prince* (New York: International Publishers, 1959), p. 137.
66. Leon Trotsky, *Stalin* (New York: Stein & Day, 1967), p. 336.
67. Rigby, p. 91.
68. Robert C. Tucker, *The Soviet Political Mind* (New York: Norton, 1971), pp. 177-79.
69. Nikita Khrushchev, *Khrushchev Remembers* (Boston: Little, Brown, 1970), p. 243.
70. Tucker, *The Soviet Political Mind,* p. 182.
71. Jeremy R. Azrael, "The Internal Dynamics of the CPSU, 1917-1967," in *Authoritarian Politics in Modern Society,* ed. Samuel Huntington (New York: Basic Books, 1970), p. 270.
72. Medvedev, *Let History Judge,* p. 15.
73. John S. Reshetar, Jr., *The Soviet Polity: Government and Politics in the USSR,* 2nd ed. (New York: Harper & Row, 1978), pp. 164-65.
74. Robert Wesson, "The USSR: Oligarchy or Dictatorship?" *Slavic Review* 31 (1972): p. 314.
75. Bernard-Henri Levy, *La barbarie à visage humain* (Paris: Grasset, 1977), p. 170.
76. Hannah Arendt, *The Origins of Totalitarianism,* rev. ed. (New York: Harcourt, Brace, 1966), p. 475.

77. Buchheim, pp. 12-13.

78. Karl H. Heller, "The Remodeled Praetorians: The German *Ordnungspolizei* as Guardians of the 'New Order,'" in *Nazism and the Common Man,* ed. Otis C. Mitchell (Minneapolis: Burgess, 1972), p. 50.

79. J.W. Wheeler-Bennett, *The Nemesis of Power: The German Army in Politics, 1918-1945* (New York: St. Martin's Press, 1964), p. 678.

80. David Schoenbaum, *Hitler's Social Revolution* (Garden City: Doubleday, 1967), pp. 65, 285, 296-97.

81. Michael Ledeen, "Fascist Social Policy," in *The Use and Abuse of Social Science,* ed. Irving Louis Horowitz (New Brunswick: Transaction, 1971), pp. 90-108.

82. George L. Mosse, *The Nationalization of the Masses* (New York: Fertig, 1975).

83. Franklin H. Littell, *Wild Tongues* (London: Macmillan, 1969), p. 78.

84. Hugh Trevor-Roper, "Introduction," in Joseph Goebbels, *The Goebbels Diaries: The Last Days* (London: Secker & Warburg, 1978).

85. Aryeh L. Unger, *The Totalitarian Party: Party and People in Nazi Germany and Soviet Russia* (New York: Cambridge University Press, 1974), p. 46.

86. Medvedev, *On Socialist Democracy,* p. 346.

87. Michael A. Merritt, "Strength through Joy: Regimented Leisure in Nazi Germany," in *Nazism and the Common Man,* pp. 61-75.

88. Daniel Horn, "Coercion and Compulsion in the Hitler Youth, 1933-1945," unpublished paper, pp. 6-7.

89. *The Speeches of Adolf Hitler, 1922-1939,* ed. Norman H. Baynes (New York: Oxford University Press, 1942), vol. 1, p. 542.

90. Daniel Horn, "The Hitler Youth and Educational Decline in the Third Reich," *History of Education Quarterly* 16 (1976): 435-36.

91. Lyttleton, p. 401.

92. De Felice, p. 31.

93. Unger, p. 42.

94. Katerina Clark, "Utopian Anthropology as a Context for Stalinist Literature," in *Stalinism,* pp. 180-98.

95.   Jean-Francois Revel, *La Tentation totalitaire* (Paris: Laffont, 1976).

96.   Schoenbaum, p. 79.

97.   T.W. Mason, "The Primacy of Politics," in *The Nature of Fascism,* ed. S.J. Woolf (New York: Vintage, 1969), pp. 176-80.

98.   Bullock, p. 158.

99.   Sidney Ratner, "An Inquiry into Nazi War Economy," *Comparative Studies in Society and History* 12 (1970): 466-72.

100. Berenice A. Carroll, *Design for Total War: Arms and Economics in the Third Reich* (The Hague: Mouton, 1968).

101. T.W. Mason, *Sozialpolitik in Dritten Reich: Arbeitklasse and Volksgemeinschaft* (Wiesbaden: West-deutscher Verlag, 1977).

102. Roland Sarti, "Fascist Reforms and the Industrial Leadership," in *The Ax Within: Italian Fascism in Action* (New York: New Viewpoints, 1974), p. 122.

103. Hildebrand, pp. 350-52, 355.

104. Franz Neumann, *Behemoth* (London: Gollancz, 1942), p. 290.

105. Barrington Moore, *Social Origins of Dictatorship and Democracy* (Boston: Beacon Press, 1966), p. 448.

106. Heinrich Winkler, "German Society, Hitler, and the Illusion of Restoration," *Journal of Contemporary History* 11 no. 4 (1976): 10; and Winkler, "From Social Protectionism to National Socialism," *Journal of Modern History* 48 (1976): 10.

107. Max Ascoli and Arthur Feiler, *Fascism for Whom?* (New York: Norton, 1938).

108. S.J. Woolf, "Did a Fascist Economic System exist?" in *The Nature of Fascism,* p. 127.

109. H.A. Turner, Jr., "Big Business and the Rise of Hitler," *American Historical Review* 75 (1969): 56-70.

110. Maxine Y. Woolston, *The Structure of the Nazi Economy* (New York: Russell & Russell, 1941), p. 12.

111. Otto Nathan, *Nazi War Finance and Banking* (New York: National Bureau of Economic Research, 1944), p. 35.

112. Schoenbaum, p. 120.
113. Irving Louis Horowitz, *Three Worlds of Development* (New York: Oxford University Press, 1966), p. 160.
114. Robert Slusser, *The Berlin Crisis of 1961* (Baltimore: Johns Hopkins Press, 1973).
115. Lyttleton, p. 187.
116. Ibid., p. 150.
117. Tannenbaum, pp. 57, 70.
118. Alberto Aquarone, *L'organizzazione dello stato totalitario* (Turin: Einaudi, 1965), p. 292.
119. Tannenbaum, p. 388.
120. Alastair Hamilton, *The Appeal of Fascism* (London: Blond, 1971), p. 67.
121. Edward Peterson, *The Limits of Hitler's Power* (Princeton: Princeton University Press, 1969); Nyomarkay, pp. 31-32.
122. Christopher R. Browning, "Unterstaatssekretaer Martin Luther and the Ribbentrop Foreign Office," *Journal of Contemporary History* 12 (1977): 313.
123. Peterson, p. 102.
124. Ibid., p. 209.
125. Paul Sauer, *Württemberg in der Zeit des Nationalsozialismus* (Ulm: Suddeutsche Verlagsgesellschaft, 1975); Karl Teppe, *ProvinzParteiStaat* (MRunster: Aschendorffsche Verlagsbuchhandlung, 1977).
126. Tannenbaum, p. 69.
127. Lyttleton, p. 165.
128. Peterson, p. 102.
129. Orlow, *1933-1945,* p. 64.
130. Helmut Krausnick, et al., *Anatomy of the SS State* (New York: Walker, 1968), p. 189.
131. Joseph Stalin, *Foundations of Leninism* (New York: International Publishers, 1939).
132. Unger, pp. 40-43.
133. Gehlen, p. 98.
134. Nikita Khrushchev, *The Last Testament* (Boston: Little, Brown, 1974), p. 137.
135. Jerry F. Hough, *The Soviet Prefects* (Cambridge, Mass.: Harvard University Press, 1969), p. 213.
136. Ibid., p. 91.

137. Ibid., p. 95.
138. Arendt, p. 475.
139. Buchheim, p. 46.
140. Ottavio Barié, "Les nationalismes totalitaires," in *L'Europe du XIXᵉ et du XXe siècle,* vol. 1, ed. Max Beloff (Milan: Marzoratti, 1964), pp. 155-228.
141. *Hitler's Table Talk, 1941-1944* (London: Weidenfeld & Nicolson, 1953), p. 142.
142. Denis Mack Smith, *Italy: A Modern History* (Ann Arbor: University of Michigan Press, 1969), p. 96.
143. Giovanni Gentile, "Il contenuto etico del fascismo," *La nazione della sers,* March 9, 1925, in Harris, p. 172.
144. Hermann Rauschning, *Germany's Revolution of Destruction* (London: Heinemann, 1939), p. 49.
145. Adolf Hitler, *Mein Kampf* (Boston: Houghton Mifflin, 1939), pp. 389-92.
146. Eberhard Jäckel, *Hitler's Weltanschauung* (Middletown: Wesleyan University Press, 1972), pp. 37-38.
147. Rudolf Binion, *Hitler among the Germans* (New York: Elsevier, 1976).
148. Adolf Hitler, p. 84.
149. David Irving, *Hitler's War* (New York: Viking, 1977), p. 509.
150. Gene Bernardini, "The Origins and Development of Racial Anti-Semitism in Fascist Italy," *Journal of Modern History* 49 (1977): 431-53.
151. Thomas Childers, "The Social Bases of the National Socialist Vote," *Journal of Contemporary History* 11 no. 4 (1976): 18.
152. Jürgen Kocka, "The First World War and the 'Mittelstand': German Artisans and White-Collar Workers," *Journal of Contemporary History* 8 no. 1 (1973): 122.
153. Peter Merkl, *Political Violence under the Swastika* (Princeton: Princeton University Press, 1975).
154. Wolfgang Sauer, "National Socialism: Totalitarianism or Fascism?" *American Historical Review* 73 no. 2 (1967): 41.
155. Ellsworth Faris, "The Landtag Election in Baden, 1929," *Central European History* 8 (1975): 164.
156. Edward R. Tannenbaum, "The Goals of Italian Fas-

cism," *American Historical Review* 74 (1969): 1183-204.

157. Ralf Dahrendorf, *Society and Democracy in Germany* (Garden City: Doubleday, 1969), p. 383.

158. Leon Trotsky, *The Revolution Betrayed* (Garden City: Doubleday, 1937), p. 278.

159. Paul Cocks, "The Rationalization of Party Control," in *Changes in Communist Systems*, pp. 154-76.

160. Khrushchev, pp. 138, 222, 226.

161. Joel C. Moses, *Regional Party Leadership and Policy Making in the USSR* (New York: Praeger, 1974), p. 154.

162. Alexander Dallin, "Bias and Blunders in American Studies on the USSR," *Slavic Review* 32 (1973): 576.

163. H. Gordon Skilling, "Group Conflict and Political Change," in Johnson, p. 221; Skilling, "The Party, Opposition, and Interest Groups in Communist Politics," in London, pp. 119-49.

164. Richard Lowenthal, "On 'Established' Communist Party Regimes," *Studies in Comparative Communism* 7 (1974): 343.

165. Hough, p. 313.

166. Joseph La Palombara, "Monoliths or Plural Systems," *Studies in Comparative Communism* 8 (1975): 325.

167. Lowenthal, p. 353.

168. George Fischer, *The Soviet System and Modern Society* (New York: Atherton, 1968).

169. Hough, pp. 281-82.

177. Medvedev, *On Socialist Democracy*, p. 37.

171. Zhores A. Medvedev and Roy A. Medvedev, *A Question of Madness* (New York: Knopf, 1971), p. 190.

172. Peter Reddaway and Sidney Bloch, *Psychiatric Terror: How Soviet Psychiatry Is Used to Suppress Dissent* (New York: Basic Books, 1977).

173. Rigby, p. 55.

174. Leonard Schapiro, *Totalitarianism* (New York: Praeger, 1972).

Index